Debunking

Myths

About Terrorism

Sol Raulson

ISBN

978-965-93121-0-8

Published 2023

To Odi my beloved

Acknowledgments

This book was written over four years. Many people helped in different ways. Some of them helped all along the way, others have helped parts. I want to thank everyone.

Thanks to Suzanne Selengut, for encouraging me to write this type of general interest politics/social sciences book.

My friends and colleagues who read parts of the book and who made useful comments: Ilan Ben Zion, Barak Nahir, Gadi Heiman, Doron Leitner, Vered Arbiv, Hanan Shai, Yuval Rothschild, Yaron Balleti, Yishai Meir, Rafi Dahan, and Shlomo Mark.

Special thanks to my friends who read the entire book for their time and attention and for giving good advice which has no doubt improved the book:

Hadas Golan, Yoel Arieli, Leah Bar, Michal Neubauer-Shani, Racheli Buzaglo, Meirav Weiser and last, my dear sister Shira Cohen.

Thanks to Haggi Roth.

Thanks to my fellow researchers - Avi Segal, Assaf Moghadam, Gadi Heiman and Mordechai Haziza — who helped to write a comprehensive book worthy of an academic perspective.

Table of Contents

Preface

People who meet for the first time tend to be interested in each other's occupation. When I reply that my academic field is international relations and specifically terrorism, the immediate response is: "So you speak Arabic!" "Why are all the terrorists Arabs?" I'm amazed. "If so, you must have studied Middle Eastern studies", they insist. "No", I reply. "Then Islam studies?" They keep trying their luck. These reactions are repeated many times and testify to the prevailing perception of terrorism: Most terrorists are Arabs, and hence I must know Arabic, have studied the Middle East and learned about Islam.

Terrorism is a phenomenon fueled by myths. After all, we all watch television, are exposed to news on TV, the Internet or in the newspapers, and know what is going on around the world. Therefore, it seems that it is clear to everyone what the state of terrorism today is, what causes it, and what is effective against terrorist organizations. The situation is not at all different among people from the mass media. They, too, repeat the same arguments and observations, until they seem to be an unquestionable truth.

At the same time, the academic discourse, which is based on thorough research, raises other, more complex, and sometimes even opposite, insights than are commonly known to the public. However, due to the gap between academic discourse and daily media discourse, academic knowledge rarely becomes part of public discourse. In practice, scholars, people in the media and the public in general speak only to the members of their groups. I understood that even though people are exposed to current information about terrorist attacks, most of them do not have a comprehensive and accurate conception of the phenomenon of terrorism. The distance between research and public discourse, especially in matters related to the personal security of every citizen, has sharpened the dual role of academia in this context: the production of knowledge and making it accessible to the public.

I started writing the book while I was equipped with these insights. Therefore, in this book, I will present the research picture on terrorism, in a fluent and accessible presentation based on academic research. As the reader will see, I will be refuting myths on terrorism. However, sometimes the researchers themselves do not agree what is the answer to the questions raised in the book, but by understanding what the complex picture consists of is a significant improvement from the daily discourse.

The public discourse is usually about non-state terrorism. People, especially in democratic countries, are less concerned with the terror of the state authorities, and this is also evident in myths, most of which concern the terror of non-state organizations. In this book, too, I will focus on the terrorist organizations rather than state terrorism.

There are many misperceptions on terrorism, but the book examines five key myths about terrorism that are often discussed in the public and media debates: the impact of globalization on terrorism, the link between poverty and terrorism, the motives of suicide terrorism, the relation of religion (and specifically Islam) to terrorism and the ability to defeat terrorist organizations. These questions will also be examined: to what extent does religion in general and specifically Islam cause terrorism? Is it possible to defeat terrorist organizations? Is the strategy of terrorism a successful one? Each chapter of the book stands on its own so that a reader who is interested in any subject is entitled to read the chapter that interests them.

The book is intended for the lay man, and therefore many discussions, research disputes, objections or expansions of studies have been inserted in the endnotes. Moreover, the book relies on many academic sources. I refer to them in the body of the book, even if I mention their insights very briefly. The reader interested in the extensive discussion can read the endnotes. Therefore, it is strongly recommended to look also in the comments.

Pleasant reading!

Is Terrorism the Dark Side of Globalization?

Just three days after the terrorist attacks on the United States on 11 September 2001, former US President George W. Bush declared: "The United States of America is fighting a war against terrorists with global deployment ... While we concentrate on the defense of America, we know that in order to defeat terrorism in today's global world we need the support of our allies and our friends."[1] In this statement, the president of the United States addressed the challenge of the terrorism that the United States was forced to confront: Its wide geographical spread and how coping with it required global cooperation. This statement, of course, was strongly influenced by the traumatic and dramatic events that took place on the soil of the United States a few days earlier, and yet what led to it recognizing that the terrorism the United States was coping with was becoming global? Why did the president of the United States link globalization with targeted terrorism toward the United States?

Globalization, Nestle and Tibetan Prayer Wheels

A few years ago, I visited Nepal. I walked the high Himalayas and visited villages of friendly and welcoming Nepalese. In the amazing landscape, we were accompanied by prayer flags waving in the wind, which were embroidered with Buddhist texts. In almost every village, there were also Tibetan prayer wheels, which believers had to rotate to disperse positive energies. The prayer wheels are cylinders with Buddhist scriptures. The scrolls were engraved with the well-known mantra: "Om Mani Padme Hum"; in other words: "Praise to the Jewel in the Lotus".

In one of the villages, we passed a series of prayer wheels. I slid my hand over them. Suddenly, when one of the prayer wheels finished half the turn, I saw a strange sight. On one side of the prayer wheel was engraved the common mantra, while on the other was the logo of the Swiss food company Nestle. A company that markets products such as Gerber baby food products and chocolate Kit-Kats was clearly visible.

Nestle was established in the middle of the 19th century, and since then has become a multi-national corporation with hundreds of factories around the world. A moment later, I realized that the Tibetan prayer wheel was made from a large container of instant coffee. How did a Swiss company's coffee barrel arrive in a remote village in Nepal, where the electricity flows only once every two days? How it became a rolling prayer? I continued to wonder as I looked around the wild landscape.

The solution to the puzzle lies in one word - globalization. The answer to my question begins about eighty years ago. In 1938, Nestlé began producing coffee powder from the "Nescafe" brand, and it led to a worldwide revolution in drinking coffee. Since the product enables rapid coffee preparation without cooking, coffee powder has become a popular product, and the company began to market its products worldwide.

Coffee is a product that can be moved relatively easily from place to place, and it can be saved for a long time, so a company that wants to market it around the world may do so relatively easily. Moreover, the commercial companies are constantly looking for new markets for their products, and today, the means of transporting large distances are faster than in the past, cheaper and more available. Hence the instant coffee, no matter what company is producing it, is a very popular hot drink all over the world, even in remote villages in the Himalayas. And so, the coffee box reached the far away village in Nepal.

It is important to remember that instant coffee, like many other products, is part of a daily and fast-drinking culture, and that the "globalization of Nescafé" is both economic and cultural. The barrel of Nescafé arrived in the village and apparently, a creative Nepalese recognized the potential of the available and convenient raw material, a tin cylinder, and transformed it into a prayer wheel. Therefore, in the photograph I took, a series of prayer wheels appeared, each engraved with a Tibetan mantra. Among them was a prayer wheel engraved with the name of a global commercial brand, a combination of a global economy and a local culture. This anecdote illustrates the processes of globalization.

It seems as if the word "globalization" has always been here, but in fact, it was used only in the last few decades. At the end of the 19th century the word "global" meant "the whole world". 1944 was the first year that "globalism" was introduced and later, in 1961, the term "globalization" was introduced into the dictionary. However, the global discourse was not part of the everyday vocabulary until the last four decades, and only in the 1980s did the terms "globalization" and "global" begin to take a prominent place in the academic, political, journalistic and business discourse.[2]

Although the word is familiar to us, it seems that many times, people cannot really explain the term globalization. As well as other social phenomena this may accommodate many definitions. Globalization is a series of processes (economic, cultural, political, transport, etc.) that erode the meaning of political borders in all aspects of life. They make our location on the globe less important than before so that often events occurring in one place affect places or people far from them.

To illustrate this series of processes, it is enough to look at the experience of visiting the mall near our home, an experience in which almost all the dimensions of globalization are presented. The mall is a kind of covered market. The economic dimension of globalization is the clearest dimension of globalization. It is reasonable to assume that almost every product we are going to buy at the mall is not locally manufactured. In the mall, we find many stores, mostly branches of global corporations, where we can purchase products that have been manufactured worldwide. If we are tired and want to eat and drink, we may visit one of the mall restaurants. Many times, these are fast food restaurants where the food is ordered quickly, delivered quickly, and eaten quickly. This is a relatively new consumer-cultural experience that characterizes our times and has spread globally. Now we can watch movies, most of which were produced in the United States. However, while we are having this cultural experience, it is also experienced by people in dozens of countries around the world at the same time with the same movie.

The shopping mall is also staffed by the mall's service workers. They clean the mall, guard it, and maintain it. Most of them are likely to be new migrant workers, people we do not really pay attention to. These people are part of a global phenomenon of migration that has changed the global labor market, and they come mainly from the global south: Africa, the Middle East, and Latin America. The shopping culture in malls is itself a product of the processes of globalization that have made this social activity global. All this is possible because a global space has been created in which the movement of people, ideas, information, and goods has become freer than in the past. It runs in a wider geographic range and is more intense than in the past.

At the same time as I write these lines, a global event is taking place, attracting hundreds of millions of people in dozens of countries all over the globe - the football World Cup. Teams from all over the world gather in one place and compete against one another. The games are broadcasted simultaneously to almost all countries in the world. Millions of people are present in different time zones, simultaneously watching one sporting event. No matter where you are, you have access to TV or the Internet, so you have immediate access to the global space and can participate in this global experience.

Until now, we have discussed the concept of "globalization" in general, but we have not yet addressed the following questions: What is the connection between globalization and terrorism? Was Bush right? Indeed, because of globalization, terrorists are scattered all over the place and may strike more easily around the world without warning? Is globalization really causing terrorism? In other words, is it because of the socio-economic reality that globalization shapes, that people turn to global terrorism? If so, what elements of global terrorism are affected by globalization - is it just the mode of employing terrorist violence or are there other aspects as well?

A pair of twins and the birth of a myth

"We're flying low. We fly very, very low. Oh! God! Too much too low!" These were the last words of flight attendant Amy Sweeney when she reported from American Airlines Flight 11, one of the two flights that crashed into the Twin Towers (World Trade Center). On September 11, 2001, at 8:00 am, American Airlines Flight 11 departed with 9 crew members and 81 passengers - 5 of them were terrorists. Fifteen minutes after departure, the plane was hijacked, and Amy Sweeney contacted Boston Airlines. She reported the stabbings of people on the plane and the kidnapping and said the kidnappers were of Middle Eastern origin. At 08:45 the plane crashed into the northern tower at the World Trade Center, and 15 minutes later another plane collided with the southern tower. At the same time, a third plane crashed into the Pentagon building, the headquarters of the US Defense Department, and a fourth plane, apparently on its way to the White House, crashed into an open field. The passengers understood that they would not survive the flight, and they tried to fight their hijackers. Nearly 3,000 people died in these events from many nationalities, and all these events had one responsible entity: Al-Qaeda.

After the attack on the Twin Towers, the understanding that terrorism poses a real threat to international security grew. A discussion began to develop on terrorism in general and on Islamic terrorism specifically. Today it takes a central place in the public and academic agenda. Many major terror attacks have reinforced the perception that there is a link between globalization and terrorism, and this misconception is slowly being accepted as common knowledge.

The prevailing perception today is that terrorism is becoming global. Many believe that the geographic range in which terrorist organizations operate is growing and that their ability to operate far from their countries of origin is improving. Such a perception of reality becomes an almost obvious reality in daily discourse.

The dominant perception is that the processes of globalization affect the violent activities of terrorist organizations, and the mistaken assumption is that as globalization processes intensified (especially after the end of the Cold War), the globalization of terrorist activity intensified. As evidence, following the terrorist attacks of September 11, 2001, a study was conducted on the media discourse in the United States, and it was found that many explicitly linked globalization to terrorist attacks: half thought that terrorism was the dark side of globalization, and about a third connected the same to global American hegemony.[3]

The belief that contemporary terrorism is more global than in the past - as a product of accelerated globalization - is not only prevalent among the media, but also among state leaders. US Secretary of State Condoleezza Rice said that this enemy is different than we have ever known. Small and evasive terrorist networks, without a state, can cause damage anywhere in the world without warning.[4] Moreover, sometimes decision-makers also make mistakes about the connection between terrorism and globalization. An example of this can be found in the words of a former Bulgarian Foreign Minister: "Terrorism is a poisonous fruit of globalization and it will be destroyed by it."[5]

It is therefore clear how in 2001, leaders, media people and others thought that terrorism is more global than ever. The events of September 11 in the United States were carried out by people who came from another part of the world - the Middle East. The leader of the organization, Osama bin Laden, was a Saudi who belonged to a family of Yemenite construction contractors. His former deputy Ayman al-Zawahiri is a doctor who came from Egypt. Bin Laden, from the moment he founded Al-Qaeda, was in three parts of the world: Afghanistan in Central Asia (in the 1980s), Saudi Arabia in the Middle East, Sudan in East Africa, and finally Afghanistan again. The main link in the group of terrorists who were recruited in Hamburg in Germany and who participated in the terrorist attacks of September 11 was that Saudi Arabia was the country of origin of most of them.

In a book published by Al-Qaeda, the organization emphasized the effectiveness of a global strategy: "In its war against the Americans, Al-Qaeda adopted a strategy based on expanding the battlefield to a [global] battlefield and weakening the enemy, his interests all over the world ... an enemy who protected only his country, understands now that he must protect his vital assets in every country."[6] Politically, Al-Qaeda is not interested in replacing the regime in a particular country, but rather aspires to wage global jihad and establish an Islamic caliphate throughout the world. Fighting the "Crusader-Jewish alliance" means that it does not direct its actions against a specific state but against other civilizations in which member states are scattered on many continents.

In 2001, Bin Laden's deputy Ayman Al-Zawahiri's discussed Al-Qaeda's global political logic: "The struggle to establish the Islamic state cannot be managed at the regional level. Clearly the crusader-led alliance led by the United States will not allow any Islamic force to take power in any Muslim country. It will use all its power to harm and overthrow such a regime. For this purpose, it will open a war front that will include the entire world."[7] This explains why some academics claimed that Al-Qaeda's approach is a byproduct of the global era.

It seems that regarding the political goals of the organization, these views have a supporting foundation. The statements mentioned above reflect mainly a state of mind and a sense of threat, and they do not rely on a systematic examination of the linkage between globalization and terrorism. This perception of the world is strongly influenced by the terrorist attacks of September 11 and by Al-Qaeda. We will then discuss the question of how Al-Qaeda represents a new phenomenon and is it the rule or the exception.

First, we will discuss the rationale behind the linkage between globalization and terrorism. According to some studies, globalization is the driving force behind terrorism, since in areas that are not part of the globalization process, the population's frustration is growing, and these areas become fertile ground for terrorism.[8] Other studies show that the core countries of the international system (rich and powerful countries both politically and militarily) acquire cheap resources and cheap manpower from peripheral countries (the poor and the weak ones), and thus bind peripheral countries to the global economy. The result is global inequality that engenders resistance movements that turn to terrorism to achieve their goals.[9]

From several studies, it appears that the description of the linkage between globalization and terrorism is even more "colorful": Globalization accelerates the vicious cycle of "dreams and nightmares." On the one hand, citizens of developing countries dream of a better quality of life in economically developed countries. On the other hand, the citizens living in developing countries, which fail in their attempts to realize their dreams, see the developed countries as an obstacle to the realization of their dreams. Thus, they export terrorism to the developed countries and hence their dreams become nightmares of these countries.[10]

Globalization leads to a new pattern of insurrection, an insurgency aided by terrorist attacks to achieve its goals. Unlike national terrorism, which is limited to a territory, a new type of insurgency, a global insurgency, takes place in several parts of the world. It is supported by minorities with the same ideology or religion and is not limited to specific geographical areas.[11]

Studies that focus on the globalization of culture indicate that due to globalization, a clash exists between values prevailing in the democratic market (the individual in the center, civil liberties and free markets) and the autocratic values of the developing countries (the rule of an individual whose authority is not limited) and collective values that are earned by them (the group in the center, a great involvement of the state in the economy and the restriction of civil liberties). The struggle between these worldviews is directed first and foremost at the United States, which represents free market civilization. The United States is also the engine of cultural globalization because American culture is spread around the world and thus "attracts fire." Terrorist organizations are not happy with the distribution of American culture because it is threatening culture in the peripheral countries of the international system. Therefore, they attack American targets and Western targets in general.[12]

According to some studies, successful terrorist attacks are a source of inspiration for radical people around the world. Terrorist organizations throughout the world imitate the ideas and methods of action of each other, leading to a global wave of terrorist attacks. The adoption of perceptions and the imitation of actions are made possible because of the globalization of information, which is the most advanced, fast and easiest manner for the distribution of ideas.[13]

Another explanation for the possible link between globalization and the globalization of terror rests on the social distance between groups: the greater the distance between the groups, the greater the likelihood of terror. In human history, there was long an overlap between social distance and geographical distance. But in the 20th century, due to globalization processes, the world has "shrank." The geographic distance no longer makes it difficult for terrorists who want to harm the citizens of the country against whom they operate.[14]

The processes of globalization enable social activity to be geographically wide, crossing borders, regions and continents. People can do so easily, quickly (and sometimes simultaneously) at a lower price than before and at a lower risk.[15] Just as for Nestlé it is easy to distribute its products around the world, to establish and acquire hundreds of factories in many countries, so for the terrorist organizations it is easier to carry out terrorist attacks in more countries.

The globalization of terrorism?

Alongside explanations about the nature of the linkage between globalization and terrorism, there are arguments that reject such a connection. It was argued that even previous waves of terror had local and transnational dimensions and that the uniqueness of today's wave is not due to globalization, but rather to the fact that Islam is the basis of its dominant ideology.[16] According to another argument, Islamic ideology is not the essence of the difference. Most of the transnational terrorist attacks in recent decades have been anti-American and directed against the United States, not because it represents the economic-cultural globalization, but because it is a superpower, which is involved in world affairs.[17]

To discuss whether globalization of terrorism is taking place and whether globalization is the cause of contemporary terrorism, we will address several secondary questions. Since Al-Qaeda carried out the major terrorist attacks that strengthened the claims about a connection between globalization and terrorism, we will first discuss the global development of Al-Qaeda. We would like to answer several questions in this context: Did the terrorist attacks of September 11 change the world of terrorism or the degree of threat it poses to us? Is globalization really leading to terrorism? Are terrorist attacks more global than in the past?

Al-Qaeda and the globalization of terrorist attacks

Al-Qaeda - the organization that after the events of September 11 became a synonym to global terrorism or global jihad - did not always have a global focus at its inception. In the mid-1980s, Abdallah Azzam, the ideological mentor of Al-Qaeda, coined the term "global jihad", a concept that over the years was the theme of Al-Qaeda. According to this view, jihad (holy war) against the infidels will no longer focus solely on Islamic regimes, because in the era of globalization it is not enough and even impossible to fight only within the borders of the territories. Jihad is required to be world-wide and to strike at the Western economy, the source of the power of the regimes in Islamic countries.[18]

Unlike Azzam's position, in the early years of Al-Qaeda, Ayman Al-Zawahiri (later bin Laden's deputy) believed that they had to fight the local regimes, especially the Egyptian regime. In 1996 Bin Laden declared that the organization's goal was to expel US forces from the Arabian Peninsula, to overthrow them from Saudi Arabia, to liberate the holy sites of Islam, and to support revolutionary Islamic movements around the world.[19] This statement reflected a kind of interim position between Azzam's position and al-Zawahiri's position. Only in 1998, a decade after the establishment of the organization, did bin Laden and Al-Zawahiri issue a joint statement about the change in the organization's order of priorities: focusing its activity on the Crusaders and Jews, and especially American targets around the world.[20]

Moreover, by 2001, the number of attacks carried out by Al-Qaeda was small and their location was in a relatively small geographical area. In the first twelve years of Al-Qaeda it carried out three successful terrorist attacks, one of which was carried out in two places at the same time. The organization's first terror attack occurred in 1995: a car bomb exploded near a facility of the Saudi National Guard; a facility run by the US military. Three years later, in the summer of 1998, the organization set up car bombs near the US embassies in Dar es Salaam and Nairobi. In October 2000, the organization attacked the US Navy destroyer, the USS Cole, while anchoring at the port of Aden in Yemen. Despite many casualties, the number of Al-Qaeda terrorist attacks in practice was very small, especially relative to the time that Al-Qaeda existed. Moreover, the organization's operating range was not global at all. The organization carried out attacks in only four countries that were relatively close: Saudi Arabia and Yemen in the Arabian Peninsula and Kenya and Tanzania in East Africa, which are also relatively close to the Arabian Peninsula.

We will now expand the scope of the analysis and examine the activities of Al-Qaeda in the years following 2001 when the organization struck worldwide. Between 2001 and 2009, Al-Qaeda and the terrorist organizations carried out terrorist attacks in 15 countries covering four continents. Indeed, an impressive global distribution. This may be evidence of Al-Qaeda's transformation from the late 1990s when it launched a global terrorist campaign. However, to know whether Al-Qaeda represents a global trend of terrorism today, it is necessary to examine the data about the global situation of world terrorism and compare its activities to other organizations.

The following table lists the terrorist organizations that carried out terrorist attacks in ten or more countries in each decade in the years 1968-2009. The distribution for decades makes it possible to compare Al-Qaeda's activity to the activities of older organizations because the organization's activities began to intensify only in the end of the 1990s.

Table 1: Organizations Operating In 10 or More Countries

Decade	Al-Qaeda *	ASALA	Fatah	PFLP	Black September	Abu-Nidal
1968-1977			11	16	22	
1978-1987		15	11			18
1988-1997						11
1998-2007	11 (15 till 2009)					

Source: RAND Database of Worldwide Terrorism Incidents.

*Including those organizations that incorporate the Al-Qaeda brand in their name, some of whom even received a "franchise" from the organization's leadership after they swore allegiance to Bin Laden or al-Zawahiri: Al-Qaeda in the Maghreb, Al-Qaeda in Arab Peninsula, Al-Qaeda in Palestine, Al-Qaeda in the Land of Two Rivers or Al-Qaeda in Iraq (its incarnation is the Islamic state – or ISIS). Other organizations affiliated with Al-Qaeda that do not use Al-Qaeda's "Brand name", did not enter the count appearing in this table, including Jum'a Islam and Lashkar a-Toiba, etc.
ASALA = The Secret Armenian Army for the Liberation of Armenia. PFLP = Popular Front for the Liberation of Palestine

From the table, we learn that Black September was the organization that carried out terrorist attacks in the largest number of countries (mainly because of a single attack in 1972, in which they were simultaneously sent 50 explosives letters to Israeli diplomatic representatives around the world). Regarding Israel, it should be noted that most of the global terrorist organizations, in terms of the global deploying of terrorist attacks, are involved in the Arab-Israeli conflict (and they are also hostile to the United States). The two organizations that are not related to the conflict directly (Al-Qaeda and the Armenian secret army for the liberation of Armenia) are hostile to Israel. In other words, over the last 50 years, Israel has fought the most global terrorist organizations.

We can learn from the comparison of Al-Qaeda with other organizations listed in the table. First, Abu Nidal and Fatah are the only organizations that have operated in 10 or more countries for over two decades. Al-Qaeda (and the organizations that bear its name) attacked only eleven countries in the decade that began its global activity. Therefore, Al-Qaeda is not a unique terrorist organization.

Moreover, Al-Qaeda is not the organization which has attacked the largest number of countries, in a given decade and in general. A comparison between the decades shows that there is no consistent increase in the number of organizations operating in many countries. In the past decade, only Al-Qaeda has operated in more than ten countries.

This analysis has implications for the question of the link between globalization and terrorist attacks. Globalization has intensified in the four decades listed in the table, while the number of organizations operating in 10 or more countries in a given decade declined. Therefore, the data show that terrorism is not necessarily the dark side of globalization.

Al-Qaeda is therefore not more global than other organizations regarding the geographic spread of terrorist attacks and certainly does not mark a new trend in the world of global terrorism. The uniqueness of Al-Qaeda stems from its global ideology and political purpose. It has a global corporate network and has carried out acts of terrorism around the world. Till ISIS was established no other organization united all these three global characteristics (global spread of attacks, global political goals and global organizational network).

The data indicate that Al-Qaeda (and its affiliated organizations) began global activity mainly in 2001. Indeed, most of the organization's activities took place after 2001. But did the terrorist attacks of 2001 mark the beginning of a new era in the field of terrorist attacks? Apparently not. In a study conducted several years after the attacks of September 11, there was no increase in the rate of terrorist attacks or the rate of victims of terrorist attacks. The change was directed at the modus operandi of terrorist organizations: terrorists were less likely than ever to kidnap hostages but used more bombs.[21] If there is no significant change in the conduct of the terrorist organizations after 2001, the question immediately arises: is Al-Qaeda the rule or exception?

The answer to this question is related to a broader question: Are the terrorist attacks more global than before? I will describe the question in other terms. If we go back to the definition of globalization, it seems that the core of globalization processes is geography. As our world becomes more global, the geography of social relations is changing. In other words, for us, the world is "shrinking". Not entirely of course, but globalization certainly affects our range of social activities: we fly easily to the edges the world, order products online from foreign countries, transfer money at the touch of a button and transmit information easily via means of communication such as TV, e-mail, WhatsApp, Twitter or Facebook. In the graph below, we will examine some selected indicators of globalization and their constant increase over the years.[22] It seems that in the recent decades, globalization has intensified almost steadily.

If there is indeed globalization of terrorist attacks, we would expect that the geographical distribution of terrorist attacks will also increase over time. We, therefore, need to examine the expansion of terrorist organizations' activity outside their countries of origin, including indications of a continuing higher rate in the number of attacks in countries outside their home regions.

Figure 1: Selected Indicators of Globalization by Year

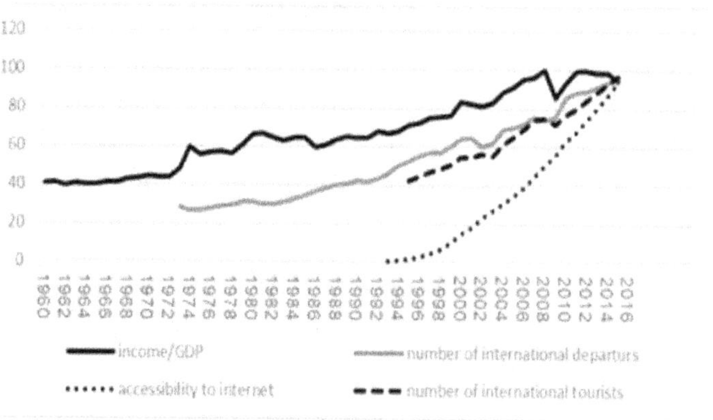

In the research literature, it is customary to divide terrorist attacks into local attacks and transnational attacks. The local attacks are carried out by a resident of the state against another local resident. In transnational attacks, the attacker and/or the victim came from different countries, or an international border was crossed, such as the hijacking of a plane on an international flight. If terrorism is a global phenomenon, then the rate of transnational terrorist attacks should be widespread and rise from year to year. But in fact, the rate of transnational terrorist attacks is very low. In the years between 1976 and 2016, the rate of local attacks (out of total attacks known for the identity of perpetrators and victims) was 80%. In other words, terrorism is overwhelmingly a local phenomenon.

Now we will turn to transnational terrorist attacks and ask: Is the absolute number of transnational terrorist attacks increasing over the years? Is the number of organizations that carry out transnational terrorist attacks increasing? Are the number of countries that have experienced transnational terrorist attacks increasing? Do terrorist organizations carry out more terrorist operations outside their own region than in the past? In other words, do they do so within global ranges as in the September 11 terrorist attacks? A positive answer to all these questions will point to the globalization of terrorist attacks. Unexpectedly, the answer to these four questions is negative. According to the statistical analysis, the rate of transnational terrorist attacks did not increase consistently from year to year.

Moreover, the proportion of countries that carried out transnational attacks decreased, the number of organizations that carried out transnational attacks each year decreased (even in the first decade of the 21st century), and the number of terrorist organizations operating outside their area of origin decreased. In fact, in most of the years and in most countries, there were no transnational terrorist attacks at all. If we were to experience globalization of terrorist attacks, we would have found a much higher rate of countries suffering from transnational terrorism, a rate that was growing steadily, but this is not the case. Apparently, Al-Qaeda is the exception that does not testify to the rule, and it is not an indication to a new trend in the world of terrorism.

In the first decade of the 21st century, however, there are de-globalization processes. If so, when was the peak period? It was in the 1980s. The table below presents the average numbers for the relevant decades (the differences Table 2 shows are reinforced by the results of statistical tests).

Why were the 1980s the peak years? This question has not yet been adequately researched, but it may be that the answer has nothing to do with globalization, but with the combination of three factors, which existed together only in the 1980s. One is the Cold War that ended in 1989, during which the Soviet Union and the Communist bloc countries supported communist (and other) terrorist organizations around the world. Another factor is the transnational Palestinian terrorism. In 1988, the level of Palestinian transnational terror activity declined after the declaration of Yasser Arafat abandoning the path of terror (however, since then, many changes have taken place, and the rate of Palestinian local terrorist attacks has increased significantly). Another factor is the Islamic revolution in Iran in 1979, which after the revolution started to support terrorist organizations (mainly Hizballah).

Table 2: Comparison between the 1980s and the Beginning of the 21st Century

	1999-2008	1979-1988
Annual average number of transnational terrorist attacks	231	313
Annual average number of terrorist organizations which perpetrated transnational terrorist attacks	36	45
Annual average number of countries in which transnational terrorist attacks occurred	40	52

So far, we have dealt with the globalization of terrorist attacks and have concluded that Al-Qaeda is the exception. Does the global jihad declared by the organization teach about the globalization of the political goals of the terrorist organizations? Here, too, Al-Qaeda belongs to a very limited group of terrorist organizations whose goals are global, and their proportion of all terrorist organizations active in recent decades it is very small.

There is one common ground to all the claims linking globalization and terrorism: there has been no systematic examination of the data. Given the data presented above, it is reasonable to assume that globalization is not related to the intensification of terrorist attacks. Several studies have shown that there is no positive correlation between globalization and the degree of global terrorist attacks. For example, a study found no relation between the rate of transnational attacks in any country and the economic globalization of the country.[23] Analysis of global trends also found no significant correlation between the variables that measure globalization and the geographical deployment of terrorist attacks.[24]

Moreover, the greater the distance between the countries of origin of the terrorists and the countries of destination, and the more obstacles (such as language), the lower the number of transnational attacks. Terrorism appears to be a local or regional threat, not a global one.[25] Also, thanks to globalization, countries that are interested in fighting terrorist organizations succeed in neutralizing many terrorist measures, and therefore, terrorist organizations do not operate around the world as easily as many tend to think.[26]

All in all, the claim that terrorism is the dark side of globalization is incorrect. This is with one caveat: it has been found that the poorer and less democratic a country is, the more likely it is that its citizens will carry out acts of terrorism outside its borders. The richer the country and the more democratic it is, the more likely it is that its citizens will become targets of transnational terrorism.

As globalization processes intensify in the countries of origin of the terrorists, the rate of terrorist attacks decreases, and it rises as the target countries are more global in economic terms. These findings can be interpreted concerning the growing global economic gaps, because people living in underdeveloped countries tend to attack the citizens of the prosperous countries. This claim has recently surfaced about the linkage between globalization and terrorism, which, according to some researchers, stems from the use of globalization for exploiting the weaker countries. Another explanation is that the killing of civilians from rich and democratic countries leads to increased media attention and helps the propaganda of terrorist organizations. Therefore, such countries are preferred targets for terrorist attacks. Another explanation is that in rich and democratic countries, it is easier to act because of civil liberties.

The processes of globalization are multi-dimensional, and their implications are complex, sometimes contradictory. Along with the claims that globalization may intensify terrorism, others suggest that globalization may moderate or reduce it. The claim that economic globalization encourages the use of terrorism is based on the notion that globalization of the economy weakens the economies of the developing countries, because it affects the weaker countries, making them even more backward or frustrating for their citizens.

On the other hand, another approach is that globalization leads to relative prosperity and equality since it allows for the flow of capital, information and new technologies to less developed countries.[27] This may actually reduce terrorism. Additionally, just as globalization is helping terrorists operate in many countries and in long distance, so it also helps countries fighting them. The advantage it gives to global action is thus reduced, so globalization in effect does not empower the geographic range of terrorist organizations.

Even Though

The sense of global threat has a certain grasp of reality regarding the intangible dimensions of globalization - the diffusion of information and ideas. Information and ideas may pass easily, quickly and simultaneously to the world, and bring three expressions in the context of globalization: the globalization of fear, the globalization of suicide terrorism and the globalization of ideological identity.

One day, on a trip I made in northern Italy, we arrived at evening to the village of Madonna di Campiglio, on the upper Dolomites. We found a place to stay, and as we registered in the lobby, I noticed that being broadcast on the television was a picture of two tall buildings and rising smoke. Fire, I thought to myself. After a while, we went out to buy batteries for my camera and noticed that the salesman was talking to two elderly women. I do not speak Italian, but from his facial expressions, the way he spoke and the words I caught here and there, I realized that he is talking about a disaster that happened in New York - a plane crashed into a building. An air accident. Pity, curiosity and empathy but not something unthinkable. Our trip continued, and with it our ignorance, but not for long: as soon as we reached the Milan airport, we encountered in the global shock wave that had recently hit the world.

For my friend, this was the first time he had travelled abroad, so he did not notice anything unusual, but I felt something was wrong, a sense of emergency drifting through the air. "Something's wrong," I told him. "What's wrong?" he wondered. "There are two soldiers here and there is tension in the air. It's not an airport atmosphere," I said. "It seems to me that there is a security incident in the field." "You're just tense," he grinned. Maybe I was, I thought. I looked for a high place from which I could see the runways and the parking space. I did not see anything special. Probably everything was in my imagination.

We continued our way to the usual route of handing over baggage, security checks and passports. Two police officers were standing at the side of the column for security inspection. My friend's handbag began to be inspected, and immediately the inspector's expression changed. She called the two policemen, and they approached to my friend and asked him to open his handbag. Inside it was a knife for spreading. His Middle Eastern appearance made it even more difficult. The security guard took the knife out with a grim expression, murmured something like "You're crazy!" and immediately threw the knife into the garbage can.

Nowadays, passengers on the airlines understand that a knife is not being transferred in a handbag, but back then, if there were no firearms or flammable or explosive items in your bag, you would have passed the security check easily. The reason for the change came to me later, when I heard that the hijackers in the September 11 attacks had used knives. Therefore, at the time, I did not have a good answer to my friend's questioner's gaze. His handbag was completely unpacked, and he, with his handbag together, inspected again under the close supervision of the police. But this was not the end of our disturbing journey to the airplane.

On the line to border control there was a disorder. Due to the careful examination and investigation, long lines were formed, people were pushing and shouting. After we passed this obstacle, it was time for boarding. I asked my friend to set aside and not join the line. "Why hurry?" I said to him, "After all, they will not take off without us". A few minutes later, it became clear that this decision was correct more than I thought. A man and a woman in uniform, wearing rubber gloves on their hands, came at random to the people waiting in line for the boarding and took them to a side room for in-depth examinations. They pulled people out of line and after a few rounds were gone.

The experience we had at the Milan airport was an expression of the globalization of fear; Feelings of anxiety, tension and fear in northern Italy, arising from events in the distant United States a few days earlier. Those who were exposed then to the media remember even today the picture of the Twin Towers burning and collapsing. Because of global TV broadcasting this was a global event, even though it took place in a defined place on Earth. Apparently, this is the real globalization of terrorism. After all, terrorist organizations do not have to carry out attacks all over the world, they just need the entire world to hear about it and be afraid. They need people in the world and decision-makers to act out of terror, and for this purpose, it is better to appear on the global news networks with horrific images of destruction, deaths and ambulances blowing sirens and rushing into the scene. The message will be delivered immediately to the world; All that is required of them is to find a target that will attract global media.

Consider the consequences of the September 11 attacks on the world of aviation: people all over the world were afraid to fly. In the decade before the terrorist attacks of September 11, 2001, the rate of departures of international flights increased from about 14.5 million at the beginning of the decade to about 22.2 million at the end of the decade. In 2002 after the well-known terrorist attacks, the rate of international flights dropped by 1.8 million, about 7% of all flights. It took two years for the aviation world to recover, and in 2004 the rate of departures returned to its previous level and even exceeded it and since then the rate of takeoffs has risen every year until the outbreak of the COVID-19 pandemic in 2020.[28]

Spreading information about murderous terrorist attacks around the world is not the only implication of the globalization of information and ideas. Since the mid-1990s, especially in the first decade of the 21st century, there has been a process of globalization of suicide terrorism: the terrorist organizations imitate each other in both direct and indirect ways. The terrorist organizations maintain direct connections and teach each other tactics of suicide terrorism. At the same time, the media are advertising attacks around the world. Such propaganda indirectly encourages their imitation, since the terrorist organizations understand that their suicide attacks have a great psychological and political impact.

The most significant factor in the global spread of suicide terrorism was Al-Qaeda. Although the organization was not the first of the terrorist organizations to use suicide terrorism, it was the first to turn it from a local phenomenon into a prominent global phenomenon (previously there were only two Hizballah suicide attacks in Argentina, far from the organization's origin, and one attack by the Tamils in India). Al-Qaeda sent suicide bombers away from their countries of origin and indoctrinated their perceptions and modus operandi to other terrorist organizations around the world. The global culture of sacrifice for the sake of God (Istishhad/martyrdom) is part of the globalization created by Al-Qaeda. This is the global nature of terrorism, not the terrorist attacks by itself.

Another cultural-ideological component - which connects to a global identity — is the idea of global jihad and the mobilization of Islamic identity in favor of that idea. Since September 11, many terrorist organizations have moved to local terrorist networks (some operating independently of Al-Qaeda or ISIS), or institutionalized organizations affiliated with Al-Qaeda or ISIS and acting out of solidarity with the idea of global jihad. The main goal is to establish an Islamic caliphate throughout the world based on the Islamic identity of the Islamic "Ummah" (community). ISIS also emphasizes the importance of establishing a state in the Middle East.

This is the ideological-identity globalization of Al-Qaeda and ISIS, who view the entire world as a battlefield, to spread their ideology. It is worth mentioning that the activities of all the organizations affiliated with Al-Qaeda or ISIS, and the local terrorist networks - which identify themselves with the global jihad - are almost entirely local, and their attacks are conducted in their countries of origin. These organizations and non-institutional networks belong to a social movement with a broad common ground: hatred of Western countries, first and foremost the United States, and support for the Salafi concept of "return to Islam". However, they do not operate according to a coherent global political strategy or a coordinated global plan. Many of these groups live in their local world according to a local political rationale, including Jabhat al-Sham (former

Jabhat al-Nusra) and ISIS, organizations who fought in the Syrian civil war against the Assad regime.

Therefore, terrorist organizations can easily recruit local activists in almost every country because of the global media, which is available and cheap. Today, terror acts in any country may be local, although they are based on global identity, and therefore the global nature of terrorism is expressed not necessarily in terrorist attacks but in ideas, in the fear that terrorism evokes in the global organizational structure. However, it seems that even these characters of globalization of terrorism are not unique since Rapaport argues that in the three waves of terrorism in the modern era that preceded the current religious wave also had transnational components.[29]

The Hunger Games
or
Does Poverty Cause Terrorism?

Poverty is one of the worst social sicknesses that have accompanied mankind since time immemorial, and probably, as the book of Deuteronomy says, will accompany humanity for many more years: "For the poor shall never cease out of the land". Poverty is one of the major causes of suffering in human life, and therefore over the years the UN has examined happiness in countries by using income level as proxy for happiness measurement.

Economic poverty is a cause of suffering that can bring one to despair, so it can be understood why decision makers believe that poverty causes terrorism. About two months after the September 11 terrorist attacks, the United Nations General Assembly presented a summary to the media about the need to cope with terrorism by addressing poverty, underdevelopment and inequality. In summary, these comments appeared: "The broad consensus on addressing terrorism went hand in hand with a recognition of the need to deal in parallel with the many concerns that had already been on the United Nations agenda…including the fight against poverty, underdevelopment, inequality, disease, and other economic and social problems."[30]

According to this position, poverty and economic inequality (income gaps) are root causes of terrorism, and in other words, terrorism is like a social disease whose expression is poverty, underdevelopment and economic inequality. Poor people are more likely than others to turn to terrorism, so countries that want to solve the problem of terrorism need to improve the living standards of their citizens and eliminate poverty. The perception is that removing poverty will discourage people from turning to terrorism and reduce the motivation of the desperate people who respond to the call of terrorist organizations. Does poverty cause terrorism? Does economic inequality lead people to resort to terrorist attacks?

Who is poor ?

During my trip to Africa, I went through several countries - each one differing in its ethnic-cultural diversity and the attractions it offered for tourists. However, some common features were visible in all these countries, including poverty, neglect and lack of physical infrastructure. Almost everywhere I traveled there were no paved, but only dirt roads. The roads were full of holes, and we felt them well as we rode the buses, which were built sometime in the middle of the 20th century and knew better times. They were battered, crowded, carrying more than twice their capacity, packed with every item people could buy on the market - from roosters to wooden rods for construction. On the way we passed hundreds of small villages: the houses in the villages are made of mud, some of which are not connected to electricity at all. The village women draw water, walking loaded with heavy water tanks and carrying a baby on their backs. Diseases such as malaria and AIDS were commonplace outside major cities; doctors and clinics were as rare as rain in the desert.

In almost every country, every city and village, two patterns are repeated, both stemmed from being a "mzungu" (white man). First, the locals saw me and my friends as a walking economic opportunity. When they examined me, they reminded me of the well-known character from the cartoon films, with the dollar symbol running in their eyes. And the other, they decided that I am rich, though in terms of developed countries I am not rich at all. I especially remember a conversation with two people in Malawi, a magical country whose residents are pleasant and hospitable. Although poor, they helped us as much as they could and hosted us in their meager home when we got stuck. "You're a rich man," one told me directly. "Why did you decide I was rich? I'm not rich at all", I replied. "You are fat, so you're rich," his friend said. "If you weren't rich, you weren't fat." "But I'm neither fat nor rich," I replied embarrassed. It is one of the moments that I realized the huge and unimaginable gap between the reality of my life and their reality. Whoever manages to purchase more food than meets his minimal needs and does not work hard physically, gaining weight, is therefore obviously a rich man. In terms of developed countries, the idea that a well-fed person is a rich person is completely unthinkable. Therefore, several questions should be addressed: Who is poor? Who is rich? A poor man is one who can't win the standard of living in the society he lives in? Or just people who do not have food?

How is poverty reflected in the World Bank global data? According to estimates by the World Bank in 2013, 10.7% of the population in the developing world lives on less than $ 1.90 a day, a 35% improvement from 1990. Data means that in 2013, 767 million people lived in poverty worldwide compared to 1.85 billion people in 1990.[31]

The poverty line is also regularly discussed in the news, and it is examined in extensive articles several times a year. Measuring the poverty line may be influenced by many approaches, and I'll not list them all here,[32] but I'll briefly mention two key approaches - absolute and relative measures of poverty. Most poverty measurement methods are based on total or relative calculation of expenditure or income. In the absolute measurement of poverty, there is a presumption that a poor person is one who cannot purchase a basic food, clothing, housing, fuel and household goods product basket. A possible measurement is estimating the rate of expenditure on food from total income. Such a measurement assumes that a poor person will devote most of their resources to basic physical needs, so most of their spending will be on food and housing. It is worth mentioning that absolute poverty, as defined by the United Nations, is an income of less than $2 per day.

Relative measurement of poverty has the assumption that people cannot be cut off from their social environment, so it is desirable to measure poverty relative to the socio-economic environment in which one lives. According to this approach, poverty is a phenomenon characterized by socio-economic inequality, so households or people whose income is substantially lower than the income of all households in the country are considered poor. Therefore, a poor person is the one who is deprived relative to the society he lives in. Different countries measure poverty in different ways, some through relative poverty and some absolute.

After discussing the question of who is poor, we will turn to these questions: Do poor people turn to terrorist activities more than the rich? How to link poverty to terrorism?

The prince and the (terrorist) pauper?

London was fifteen hundred years old, and was a great town…The streets were very narrow, and crooked, and dirty, especially in the part where Tom Canty lived, which was not far from London Bridge. The houses were of wood, with the second story projecting over the first, and the third sticking its elbows out beyond the second…The house which Tom's father lived in was up a foul little pocket called Offal Court, out of Pudding Lane. It was small, decayed, and rickety, but it was packed full of wretchedly poor families. Canty's tribe occupied a room on the third floor. The mother and father had a sort of bedstead in the corner; but Tom, his grandmother, and his two sisters, Bet and Nan, were not restricted—they had all the floor to themselves, and might sleep where they chose…"[33]

This description is taken from Mark Twain's book, The Prince and the Pauper. The heroes of the story are Tom, a poor boy, and Edward, a prince of the British royal house. The two of them were interchangeable with each other, and Twain presented to us the difficulties each had in his new life. The paragraph quoted embodied the extreme poverty that many Londoners inherited in the 16th century. Twain's description conveys the sense of poverty, more than any other numerical definition and measurement. The reader is well able to understand how hard poverty is, and the suffering and desperation of extremely poor people.

Moreover, the contrast between poverty and the comfortable life and high standard of living in the royal palace is particularly shocking. If everyone suffers from a shortage, this is probably the reality of life, and there may be nothing to do, but if any group in the population enjoys abundance and luxury, the poor person realizes that one can live differently. If he does, he feels that the group with resources exploits the weaker group, and the meaning of poverty is even more acute for him. From that, it will make it easier for the reader to understand that people living in such a situation may feel that they have been pushed to the margins of society, that they are being exploited, that no one cares, and they have nothing to lose. They will be prepared to take extreme and violent measures to shout their grievances and change their situation, including using terrorist attacks.

In 1998, the United Nations assembly defined the sense of poverty:

"Fundamentally, poverty is a denial of choices and opportunities, a violation of human dignity. It means lack of basic capacity to participate effectively in society. It means not having enough to feed and clothe a family, not having a school or clinic to go to, not having the land on which to grow one's food or a job to earn one's living, not having access to credit. It means insecurity, powerlessness and exclusion of individuals, households and communities. It means susceptibility to violence, and it often implies living on marginal or fragile environments, without access to clean water or sanitation."[34]

In this definition, the social and emotional implications of poverty are discussed:

Breach of respect, insecurity, inability to manage a family economy, social exclusion and violence. The emotional aspects of poverty are one of the links between poverty and violence, because experiencing poverty can push the individual into violent activity: poverty causes despair and frustration, which cause anger, and anger leads to violence. Now the claim is raised by the UN assembly on poverty as a fertile ground for terrorism. In an interview with the London Times, Abd al-Razak, Hamas's former finance minister, threatened: "Given the difficult economic situation in the Palestinian Authority and the freeze of US and European aid to the Palestinian Authority, and the Israeli tax freeze - Israel is likely to face increasing [terrorist] attacks. Relations with Israel will not remain so calm. I'm sure of it. I am not saying that we as a government will be pushing in this direction, but starvation, economic problems and non-payment of salaries will be most manifest in opposition and security issues."[35]

In the global discourse, an economic analysis of the situation in the Palestinian Authority leads to the conclusion that a poor (or worsening) economic situation leads to a wave of terrorist attacks. However, Abd al-Razak referred his claims to the people of the liberal Western countries, who donate money to the Palestinians, explaining that the roots of terrorism lie in poverty and economic danger. Apparently, his claims often do not fall on deaf ears - many believe that terrorist attacks on Israel are due to the economic pressure on Palestinians and their poverty and that Israel is indirectly responsible for the deterioration of the security situation. In the opinion of many, due to the economic stress, the poverty and the Palestinian shortage are turning their anger on those who they think are the main reason - the State of Israel. Journalist Danny Rubinstein also came to a similar conclusion about the link between poverty and terrorism from the Gaza Strip:

"A personal experience taught me years ago an important lesson on the economic situation in the Gaza Strip. This happened before the Six Day War. As a young soldier, I took part in ambushes on the Gaza Strip to catch infiltrators. One night my friend noticed a close-up figure, shot and hit her, and at dawn, we found out that we had hit and killed a barefoot Arab boy which was wearing worn cloths. He was holding a pack of ropes from his hand, the ones that are used to tie hay bales. One of us looked at the dead man and asked the commander: "He had infiltrated and was killed for collecting ropes? What would he do with them?" The commander was amazed at the question and answered that he probably would have sold them in the Gaza market. Since 1948, the Gaza Strip has been a poor piece of land, with crowded refugee camps in the southern coastal lowlands. No wonder Gaza is different from the West Bank, and it is the one that has carried out most of the Palestinian terrorist organizations that continue to attack us today."[36]

There are two explanations for the link between poverty and terrorism in the research literature: One is rational

50

calculations, which see human beings as economic players, and the other - the relative deprivation of the poor. According to the economic argument human beings are rational, and in their decisions, they define the cost, the benefit, and the opportunities before them. They will turn to the practice of terrorism after weighing all these components, so that turning to terrorism will be determined by the degree of cost-benefit balance. According to the economic-rational theory, when the resources available to man are limited and he is required to select an alternative out of several - the best alternative for him is to be calculated according to the degree of loss not choosing the other alternatives. In other words, people will choose the alternative that benefits the most.

If turning to terrorism is indeed rational, then the use of terrorism is an alternative among several alternatives available to the person. According to the opportunity-cost theory, participation in acts of terrorism stems from the rational and clear preferential treatment of terrorism over nonviolent political protest. Those who recruit to terrorist organizations and their managers weigh the opportunities and cost of using violence.

The environment is also required to consider both the economic cost and the social, economic and political gains that may be made in supporting a terrorist organization. An environment that supports the terrorist organization by providing hiding and intelligence helps it survive. When such an environment is required to choose between terrorism and other alternatives, it is easier to participate in terrorist acts. Environment as such increases chances of social profits due to participation in acts of terrorism and the risk for the organization launching terrorist campaign is not high.

The same is true in the context of poverty and terrorism. If a person has no expectation that his/her financial future will be better and thinks that they will have the opportunity to change the economic situation, terrorist organizations can recruit him/her into their ranks much more easily; the profit in turning to terrorism will be higher than the cost. If so, in poorer countries it is more likely that more terrorist attacks will occur. Although the cost of engaging in nonviolent activity is lower than engaging in violent activity, sometimes engaging in terrorism averts terrorist activists' mental profit. People may gain social solidarity and high social status for themself and their family, such as the martyrdom in Islamic terrorism.[37] Sometimes even financial gain may be a consideration, as in cases of profits in the Israeli-Palestinian conflict, where terrorist operatives know that if they will be killed, their family will receive money. In this situation it is worth mentioning failed states – states that have a low level of development in terms of GDP per capita, literacy and life expectancy[38] are less successful coping with terrorist organizations.[39]

Their citizens are poor and their ability to charge a high cost to terrorist operatives is limited. Hence such countries are likely to suffer from increased terrorist activity, or alternatively they will export more terrorist operatives compared to developed countries. Another explanation, concerning the connection between socio-economic factors and turning to terrorism, focuses not on absolute poverty but on relative poverty. Relative poverty is often measured by income inequality. According to this approach, an approach of "relative deprivation," political violence and terrorism occur when there is no alignment between the standard of living that a person expects to achieve and the standard of living that he has in practice. Thus, poor economic conditions such as low incomes will provoke frustration, and frustration will increase the likelihood of resorting to violence.[40] Moreover, people who believe that others limit their financial opportunities will be even more frustrated and likely to turn to terrorism. Thus when a particular group of the general population is discriminated against, such as an ethnic or religious minority, a social protest aimed at achieving equal rights with the majority or separation from the state may arise.

According to these claims terrorism is an extreme reaction to a socio-economic situation. However, the lack of satisfaction itself does not necessarily lead to terrorism. An essential component on the way to terrorism is also the feeling that an injustice has been done to the individual or group and that the responsible entity is recognized (such as the government).[41]

Hence under poor economic conditions it will be easier to recruit people for terrorist activities or to raise donations for terrorist organizations. However, an examination of terrorist activity as in West Germany - "the Red Army faction" - Japan - "the Japanese Red Army" - and Italy "the Red Brigades", shows that the members of the upper classes are those who turned to terrorism and not the lower classes. If so, does poverty and economic inequality increase terrorism? Do the poor mobilize for terrorism more than the rich?

How to examine the question of the connection between poverty and terrorism?

When examining the relations between poverty and terrorism, we can use three levels of analysis:

Assessing the economic situation of those recruiting for acts of terrorism.

Comparing several districts in one country or comparing several countries over time.

Analyzing the global level of the link between poverty and terrorism.

Most studies measure terror using the number of terrorist attacks annually in a country. Usually in studies on the relation between poverty and terrorism, poverty is measured by domestic Gross Domestic Production (GDP) per capita. The GDP per capita of the countries is the calculation of total products and services produced during a defined way all in one year. This value is divided by the size of the country's population. The assumption is that if the GDP per capita is low, then the state is poor. In fact, this method measures the degree of wealth of the state and not the degree of poverty, because the GDP per capita is higher, so the country is richer.

To examine the question of whether poverty causes terrorism requires us to examine if indeed there are relations between poverty and terrorism, in other words, to ask whether if a country (or a particular district) is poorer, the number of terrorist attacks is higher? This is a linear connection. The linear connection can be positive when if the value of one variable is getting higher, also the values of the other variables are getting higher. The relationship can also be negative if when the values of one variable are getting lower, the values of the second variable are higher.

Regarding the connection between poverty and terrorism, the expectation is for a negative relation: when a state or a district would be less rich, i.e., have a lower GDP per capita, the number of terrorist attacks are expected to be higher.

It should be noted that in some of the studies in which such a connection is examined a distinction is made between local terrorism, in which only people from the same country participated in terrorist attacks, and terrorism that crosses countries in which the attacker and victim are from different nationalities. Although today, in the era of globalization of mass communication when many times even domestic terrorist attacks are affected by global identities, the distinction between local and transnational terrorism is still significant for understanding the nature of the relationship between poverty and terrorism: local terrorism affected mostly by domestic conditions (such as poverty) and transnational terrorism affected by both domestic conditions in the origin country of the terrorists and/or victims.

More poverty = more terrorist attacks[42]

Osama Bin Laden was the most famous terrorist in the world, and he founded one of the most famous terrorist organizations in recent decades. There is no clear answer to the question of how much money Bin Laden had: estimations range from few million dollars to a billion dollars.[43] In any case, Bin Laden was probably not poor and may even have been the richest among leaders of terrorist organizations, if you do not consider terrorists who amassed wealth while running terrorist organizations (e.g., Yasser Arafat). However, the most important information is that bin Laden came from a wealthy family of contractors who lived in Saudi Arabia. Often such examples are proof that terrorists are not poor.

Is bin Laden the exception? Or are only the junior members of the organization poor and the leaders of the organization rich? Is there a relation between the poverty of a state or province to the extent of terrorist attacks? If there is indeed a relation between poverty and terrorism, it is observed that in rich countries there will be fewer terrorist attacks compared to poorer countries. It will be expected that, from a global perspective, it seems that the group of rich countries as a whole, suffers less from terrorist attacks compared to the group of poor countries.

Some studies have found a linear relation between poverty and terrorism.[44] One of them is the research of Kwan Li and Drew Schaub which focused on the member countries of the Organization for Economic Co-operation and Development (OECD) and examined whether the number of terrorist attacks in these countries, which are relatively rich, was lower than the number of terrorist attacks in the countries in the rest of the world.[45] The OECD is an organization of 35 countries, including, for example, the United States, Chile and the United Kingdom. When it was founded only European countries were members, but now countries from all over the world are members of the organization. States of the organization include both countries that are developed in terms of economic or associated countries which recently experienced great economic growth. These are countries whose economies are growing and are about to take a prominent place in the global economic arena. The organization is an international forum, and its member states develop common economic and social policies. The OECD goals are to support economic and environmental growth, encourage employment, raise standards of living, and assist in global economic development. If indeed poverty causes terrorism, it is expected that among the group of member states in the OECD, which are economically developed countries, the occurrence of terrorist attacks is lower than the number of terrorist attacks in countries that are not OECD members.

Li and Schaub examined two contradicting hypotheses: One hypothesis was that economic globalization — measured by the volume of international trade in a country and by the volume of foreign direct investment in the country and the flow of capital into it — promotes terrorism. Another hypothesis was that economic globalization reduces the number of terrorist attacks. For the discussion about poverty and terrorism, this hypothesis is important, based on the assumption that economic globalization promotes the material development of countries, and that economic development reduces terrorist attacks.

The researchers studied 112 countries in 1975-1997 and found that when the GDP per capita was lower in a specific country, the number of transnational terrorist attacks was higher. It means that in poor countries more terrorist attacks take place. But Li and Schaub also tested all OECD member countries as a group. They also checked if a group of economically developed countries suffered less from terrorist attacks compared to countries that were not members of the organization.

They found that in the OECD member states the number of transnational terrorist attacks is lower. Moreover, even when they examined the two variables together, the degree of economic development and membership of the organization, the results did not change.[46]

Is more poverty = more terrorist attacks?

Despite studies that indicate the relationship between poverty and terrorism, in the scientific literature the predominant claim is that the relation between poverty and terrorism is not significant. As evidence, one of the studies found a relationship between poverty and terrorism, but there was no association between unemployment, an economic scarcity induction and the number of terrorist attacks.[47] A second study found that terrorist organizations which have their homeland in poorer countries do not succeed in recruiting many activists and they are not bigger than terrorist organizations which have their home in richer countries.[48] Another study found an association between inequality and the high prevalence of terrorist attacks, and the same study also found support for the opposite claim. They found that as GDP per capita was higher there were more terrorist attacks.[49]

If so, the picture that emerges from the research literature is different from the common claims in the public and media discourse. For the most part the prevailing view is that poverty necessarily causes terrorism; however, there is very little empirical confirmation of this view, although "the scroll cannot yet be closed"[50] on this claim.

A review of a study that surveyed the causes of terrorism revealed that studies supporting the claim that terrorism is related to poverty are few; the number of studies that did not find evidence for such a relationship is at least twice as large.[51] For example, a Meta-Analysis[52] assessment of 13.4 million statistical analysis that tested 65 possible causes of terrorism found 18 factors significantly associated with terrorism, but did not find a relation between GDP per capita (as mentioned, the proxy for poverty) and the number of terrorist attacks.[53]

In another study several economic variables, including poverty and economic inequality, were examined and it was found that they are not predictors of terrorism.[54] Yet, other characteristics of countries - such as the size of the population, the degree of ethnic and religious diversity and oppression by the state - were related to terrorism.[55] Another study examined the relationship between poverty and terrorism (local and transnational terrorism) and found that when other characteristics of the countries were also considered, such as the degree of political freedom in the country, the likelihood of terrorist attacks occurring in poor countries was not significantly higher than in other countries.[56] Also, a study which focused on European countries found no correlation between poverty and local terrorism, after controlling for other alternative explanations.[57] For the last example – a study which compared provinces in India also returned similar results: the poorer provinces in India were not more terror-stricken than the wealthy ones.[58]

Poverty and the global map of terrorism

It seems that worldwide poverty has decreased by about 50% in the last few decades and has decreased steadily year by year. In contrast, the rate of transnational terrorist attacks and the number of victims in these attacks has changed a lot (it increased in the 1980s, decreased in the mid-1990s and rose again at the beginning of the 21st century). Economic inequality worldwide, as measured by GDP, has grown steadily from the 1970s. Economic inequality reached its peak in the 1990s, but as mentioned in those years transnational terrorism decreased.[59]

Similar findings come up when examining specific regions of the world. We expect that if there is a link between poverty and terrorism, the poorest regions of the world will suffer from a greater rate of attacks compared to the richer regions. It is surprising to find that sub-Saharan Africa, the poorest region in the world, suffered the lowest rate of terrorist attacks and the rate of casualties there was the lowest. In contrast the Middle East, a region as poor as Africa, suffered higher rates of terrorist attacks and victims. (Regions with the medium level of economic development suffered the highest terrorist attacks). Moreover, a larger number of terrorist organizations are active in the most economically developed states in the world, especially in Western Europe and North America, while in Africa south of the Sahara, the number is almost the lowest of all the regions in the world. Therefore, these findings do not confirm the link between poverty and terrorism.

This is true also about economic growth: among the 29 countries which saw their economies shrink in 1990-2005, in 17 there were no terrorist attacks, and in eight of the countries the terrorist attacks rate was lower than the worldwide average. In contrast, countries that suffered from a high rate of terrorist attacks were in all sorts of degrees of economic growth. Hence, a slowing economy is not necessarily related to terrorism.[60]

So far, we discussed the question of whether in poorer territories - regions, states or provinces - more terrorist attacks occur, or the likelihood of terrorist attacks is higher? Another angle, interesting and even more intuitive, may be the terrorists themselves. Is it true that anyone who participates in terrorist activities is poor? Are terrorists poorer relative to the society they live in? If so, is poverty the cause of terrorism?

The legend of the poor terrorist

Research on the social background of terror operatives began several decades ago. These studies examined the Basque underground (ETA),[61] members of the "Red Brigades",[62] and several terrorist groups in the Middle East, Japan, Latin America and Western Europe.[63] All studies found that members of terrorist organizations were not inclined to come from the lower socio-economic layers of society.

When examining profiles of Islamic terrorist operatives, for example global jihad operatives, it was found that they do not come from an economically poor background, which allegedly was supposed to explain the hostility towards the United States.[64] Moreover, a survey conducted in 14 countries, representing about

62% of the world's Muslim population, found that only among city dwellers was support for Islamic terrorism related to poverty or lack of income satisfaction.

Michael Mousseau, who conducted the survey, explained that many of the poor in cities came from the villages, and they continued to embrace the values and traditions of the village, while the elite in the cities were secular and modern, so the poor in the cities saw them (and the Western countries that represent these values) as the enemies of Islam. The imams in the mosques use these perceptions and recruit the poor of the cities into their ranks.[65] Therefore, it is possible that the poor people in the big cities are mobilizing for terrorist activity not necessarily because of poverty but because of cultural and religious values that they hold.

To establish the socio-economic characteristics of the terrorists, I will examine in detail two studies that discuss the question of the connection between poverty and terrorist activity: one in the context of the Israeli-Palestinian conflict and the other in the context of the Israel and Hezbollah conflict. The researchers analyzed the social background of the activists of Hezbollah, Hamas, Palestinian Islamic Jihad, and a small Jewish underground group which was active for few years in the late 1970s and the 1980s. They also examined the relationship between terrorism and the Palestinian economy up to the outbreak of the second Intifada uprising in September 2000.

The two American scholars, Alan Kruger and Gitka Malkova,[66] based their work on public opinion polls conducted by the Palestinian Center for Policy and Survey Research in December 2001, in which 1,357 Palestinians from Judea, Samaria and the Gaza Strip participated. Participants were asked for their views on the armed struggle against Israel, support for an agreement between Israel and the Palestinians, the terrorist attacks on September 11, 2001, and more. These were the days of the second Intifada, and of course, most respondents supported armed attacks against Israel. Many of the Palestinians supported terrorist attacks against civilians even in the sovereign territory of Israel (not only in Judea, Samaria and Gaza Strip) and thought it may help the Palestinians more in the negotiations with Israel. This support was widespread among the poor and rich Palestinians.

Moreover, in other surveys conducted in Judea, Samaria and the Gaza Strip - in July and August 1998, September 1999 and February 2000 - respondents were asked about their financial situation in the last three years and the expectations for the future. For example, participants were asked if they thought the future would be better and how optimistic they were about their financial future. The aim was to examine whether a change in economic expectations was related to a change in Palestinian terrorist activity. It turned out that the Palestinian public believed that their economic situation improved in the three years before the Intifada, i.e., from 1998 to 2000, and these findings are consistent with the decline in the rate of unemployment during this period. If so, it seems that the outbreak of the second Intifada, a few months after the last survey, was not due to the aggravation of the economic situation or from a sense of despair in the wake of the economic situation.

Eli Horowitz, an Israeli researcher, provided Kruger and Malkova with biographical data on 129 members of Hezbollah's military wing who were killed in 1982-1994.

The data were taken from articles about the organization's casualties, articles published in Hezbollah's weekly magazine. An analysis of the dead activists' backgrounds revealed that the rate of poverty among Hezbollah casualties (28%) was lower than the poverty rate in the general population of Lebanon (33%). Kruger and Malkova conducted statistical tests on the demographic characteristics of Hezbollah's dead activists and concluded that there was no connection between poverty and mobilization to the armed wing of Hezbollah.[67]

However, the question of mobilization for Hezbollah is a little more complex. A follow-up study, based on Kruger and Malkova's data, examines the link between poverty and education and terrorism among Hezbollah recruits and it also found that the recruits were not poorer than the others in the Lebanese society, but they found another interesting result: poverty was shown to be related to participation in terrorist violent only among those with an academic education. They are the ones who are more likely than others to enlist in a terrorist organization. Apparently, terrorist organizations recruit educated people, as they may be more talented activists than others.[68]

Alan Krueger and David Laitin examined whether the relationship between poverty and terrorism is conditioned on the extent of education, and it is possible that the reason researchers do no find relationships between poverty and terrorism is related to the desire of terrorist organizations to recruit also among the affluent population.[69]

What about the Jewish underground that operated in Judea and Samaria in the late 1970s and 1980s? The activists in the underground were Jews, most of them were educated, and they were no poorer than the general Jewish population. They had good jobs and were even well-paid professionals, such as teachers and engineers.

In another study, Claude Berrebi examined the biographies of 283 Palestinian fatalities in terrorist attacks, which were published in the magazines of Hamas, Palestinian Islamic Jihad and the Palestinian Authority in 1997-2002.[70] The study showed that usually the perpetrators of Palestinian attacks in general and the suicide bombers in particular did not come from poor families. During the study period, 31% of Palestinians were defined as poor, and only 16% of the perpetrators of the attacks were defined as poor. Moreover, 31% of the general Palestinian population were unemployed, and only 6% of the terrorist operatives that Berrebi had employment information about were unemployed. If we focus on the perpetrators of the suicide bombings, we will find that only 13% were poor, while in the Palestinian population aged 16-50, 32% were poor. Even when other variables were examined - such as age, place of residence and marriage - a similar finding to Kruger's and Malekova's study emerged – a negative relation between poverty and terrorism. That is, the probability that a poor Palestinian will participate in terrorist activities is lower than the probability that a non-poor Palestinian will participate in such activities. Therefore, it is possible that the connection between poverty and terrorism is different than the usual take in the public discourse. If so, could it be that in poorer places fewer terrorist attacks occur?

The complex links between poverty and terrorism

Allegedly, the link between poverty and terrorism is simple. However, I will present now several studies indicating complex and surprising relations of poverty to terrorism. At core, it was found that the connection between poverty and terrorism may stem from the question of who is to blame for economic shortage? It was found that it is not poverty per se that causes terrorism but economic differences among groups in the population and intentional economic discrimination.[71] This is true even regarding domestic terrorism that is affected by the deliberate discrimination of minority ethnic groups than from the economic situation in the country.[72]

When you think of the causal mechanism linking poverty to terrorism it seems logical. Imagine a person living in a poor country who is not knowledgeable of any other reality. Everyone around him is poor, and in other cities in the country the situation is similar. Will the poor turn to political violence or even non-violent protest? Probably not, since this is the reality of their life and of the lives of those around them. The situation is fundamentally different if the poor belong to a poorer group in the population, which is discriminated against compared to other groups in the population. In such a case the poor are likely to turn to violent protest the government and may even carry out terrorist attacks.

The complex relations between poverty and terrorism have been examined in two studies. The three researchers - Walter Enders, Gary Hoover and Todd Sandler[73] - analyzed both transnational and the domestic terrorist attacks. Their findings may shed light on the complex relations between poverty and terrorism and help to understand the cause of non-consistency in previous findings regarding the connections between poverty and terrorism. In their first study, Enders, Hoover and Sandler found that poverty has a strong linkage to local terrorism, but the statistical relation is not linear:[74] In poorer countries there are more terrorist attacks than in richer countries. However, in rich countries an increase of GDP does not reduce the number of terrorist attacks. Moreover, the critical point is US$1000 per capita. Over the level of a GDP per capita of US$1000 the rate of terrorist attacks decreases considerably. The findings about the transnational terrorist attacks are similar and the impact of GDP per capita on the rate of terrorist attacks is smaller. Also, the relations between poverty and terrorism are not linear, but has an inverse U shape. That is, as the GDP per capita increases, terrorism increases (up to the level of income of US$2215), and then as the GDP per capita increases, the number of terrorist attacks declines. In such a situation, anyone who seeks a linear connection, that is, an increase in the number of terrorist attacks as the country is poorer, will not find any significant statistical connection between poverty and terrorism.

The researchers explain that the relationship between poverty and terrorism is not linear because the higher the rate of GDP per capita rises, the resources available to terrorist organizations also rise, so that to some extent the GDP per capita will increase terrorism. However, over a certain level of GDP per capita participants of potential terrorist attacks must sacrifice much to participate in terrorism, and therefore calculating cost and benefit they are less likely to join terrorist organizations. Also, the government may distribute more resources to all groups of the population within it, so that it softens complaints against the government and reduces the need to turn to violence. Furthermore, with the increase in GDP per capita the government manages to suppress terrorist organizations or secure potential targets for terrorist attacks better than before.

In a follow-up study, Anders, Hoover and Sandler examined the non-linear relationship between terrorism and poverty as a function of time. As mentioned, it is the countries with medium incomes that suffer more than the others from terrorism. But from the 1990s, when religious terrorism intensified, the situation has changed, and today countries with low GDP are suffering more than others from terrorist attacks. The change is reflected both in the location of the attacks and in the countries of origin of the perpetrators of the attacks. By 1993 only 24% of transnational terrorist attacks occurred in the poorest countries, but after 1993, 61% of transnational terrorist attacks occurred in the poorest countries. As well in the period before 1993 the perpetrators of terrorist attacks usually came from the medium-high economic status countries. In contrast, after 1993 the perpetrators of terrorist attacks are from poorer countries. The explanation for this is changes from 1990s, since more terrorist organizations are religious and less leftist (leftist organizations advocated for equal economic rights and fought in the name of the lower economic classes).

In the 1970s and 1980s there were leftist terror groups mainly in rich countries, while religious terror groups operated mainly in the Middle Eastern countries, North Africa and Asia, which generally are poorer countries.

From the early 1990s, religious terrorist organizations targeted their attacks against available targets in their countries. Moreover, after the terrorist attacks of September 11, 2001, the security measures were tightened, so the terrorist organizations directed their efforts to the poorer countries, where the security measures were less rigorous.

Summary

Most studies found no correlation between poverty and terrorism, namely no evidence to the widespread claim that as the country is richer it will suffer less terrorist attacks. Apart from some evidence related to suicide terrorism, there is also no evidence that the poor people of society are the ones who join terrorist organizations. Moreover, the mere finding of a statistical correlation between the degree of poverty of the country or the province and any rate of terrorist attacks do not necessarily show that people turned to terrorist activity due to economic scarcity. That is, terrorist attacks did not necessarily result from suffering and frustration, or from cost effect calculations.

Regarding the explanations of the researchers mentioned above, it seems that poverty is not a direct factor leading to terrorism. Thus, for example, Enders, Hoover and Sandler claim that until the 1990s transnational terrorist attacks were perpetrated in relatively rich countries because the Marxist ideology of terrorist organizations made the rich countries targets, even if the perpetrators of the terrorist attacks themselves were not necessarily poor people. Later there was an increased number of transnational terrorist attacks in poor countries, in part because after the terrorist attacks on 11 September 2001, stricter security measures in the West made it harder to implement terrorist attacks in those countries. In addition, an increase in GDP reduces poverty and enables the state to provide economic benefits. It also enables the state to invest resources in the war on terrorist organizations and to defend attractive targets from terrorists, so that terrorist attacks in its territory may be reduced.

If so, it seems that the prevailing perception that poverty is necessarily the cause of terrorism in the best case is standing on a shaky ground. If indeed there is a connection between poverty and terrorism it is complex, varying over time and not standing by itself as a single cause. The simplistic version - poverty = more terrorist attacks - is misleading and gives rise to incorrect statements. One of them is from the Swedish Minister of Education who responded to Hamas rockets attacks on Israel in summer of 2014: "Social discrimination, unemployment and hopelessness. A perfect breeding ground for hatred and extremism."[75] The complex relationship between poverty and terrorism is related to other factors, such as education, religion and the political situation. All of these affect the phenomenon of terrorism and can sometimes explain terrorist attacks no less well than poverty and perhaps even more. In the next chapter we will therefore deal with the connection between religion and terrorism.

Are All Terrorists Muslims?

There is now a widespread perception that Islam is the source of terrorism in the world. The connection between terrorism and Islam is clear and obvious and it is perceived as a solid belief. In a pamphlet I received one day it was written: "I guess doctoral students all over the world are already 'making a living' from terrorism research and debating about theses and sub-definitions…what is missing is a simple sentence: You said terrorism? You said Islam! [76] Indeed?

This chapter discusses the myths concerning the relationship between religion/culture and terrorism. I will examine some common questions in this regard - is the relationship between religion and terrorism what appears in recent decades only? Nowadays, religion is the main factor driving terrorism. Are we really experiencing a "clash of civilizations" as claimed by Samuel Huntington? Are Islamic terrorist or generally religious organizations deadlier than non-religious terrorist organizations? If so, why? Are all terrorists Muslims? Is terrorism an integral part of Islam?

Terrorism and religion: Is anything new under the sun?

Often, studies of terrorism refer to "new terrorism" and "old terrorism". Old terrorism is usually local and takes place in a particular country due to domestic political disputes. Old terrorist organizations use violence to convince their enemies to join the negotiation table, recognizing their legitimacy and talking with them. In contrast, the "new" terrorist organizations are waging a global war against forces of evil. Many times, these religious organizations are not limited by political considerations, such as maintaining the support of broad population groups, and are willing to act with great violence and cause a lot of damage and the loss of many lives. This is how an organization like Al-Qaeda behaved, and it is a prominent representative of the new terrorism. [77]

However, religiously motivated terrorism has been documented since ancient times. Until the 19th century, the justification for using terrorism was mainly religious.[78] Modern terrorism, on the other hand, has a variety of reasons: anarchism, socialism, nationalism, ethnicity, the economy, occupations, and religion. The two most famous religious terrorist organizations that operated in antiquity were the Sicariks and the Hashashin. In this chapter I will elaborate a little on a third terrorist organization, less familiar, the Thugs. This is one of the biggest religious terrorist organizations to have ever been documented. Even today the name is a synonymous to the word "bully" in English. It is not certain that the Thug organization accurately answers the term "terrorist organization" because today the term contains political aims and meanings. However, the Thugs murdered unarmed civilians to achieve their religious objectives. The Thugs organization was an Indian cult of assassins who worshiped the Hindu goddess Kali, and as part of the religious worship strangled to death their victims, mostly travelers. No one knows how many victims the Thugs murdered, but according to conservative estimates, in modern times alone, the Thugs murdered about a million people! Even if we reduce the number into a half still the number of victims is enormous, certainly relative to the victims of terrorist attacks nowadays - hundreds of dead or several thousand for the most.

The main reason for the high rate of murders was their prolonged activity over centuries. Their activity was driven by a religious conception and was not directed against the social or governmental institutions, but against individuals. That is different from most terror organizations, which threaten the existence of the sociopolitical status quo or wish to preserve it.

The members of the organization did not threaten the Indian political institutions. According to Hindu mythology, a giant monster devoured humans the moment they were created, but Kali killed it. From every drop of the monster's blood a demon was created, and from every drop of blood of the demons killed by Kali a new demon was created. Kali solved the problem by licking their blood.

The members of the sect believed that Kali created two peoples from her sweat who helped her by struggling with the demons using handkerchiefs that she was wearing. Thus, Kali succeeded in killing the demons without shedding their blood and prevented them from reproducing themselves. After completing their mission, she commanded that the people must keep the handkerchiefs and pass them on to their children.

Hindus believe that the goddess Kali represents the power of the universe, the power of existence and the destruction of life together, and that she is the goddess of time managing the endless circles of life. The Thugs believed they had to supply the blood that the goddess Kali needed. Hence, each of them is required to save his life as much as possible for so that he can continue to kill and thus maintain the cosmic balance. According to estimations, each member of the cult killed an average of about 3 people each year. The Thugs burgled the property of their victims, but their main interest was in the killing itself. They deliberately extended the dying time of their victims to let Kali have plenty of time to enjoy the victims' sense of terror. After the deaths of the victims, they bribed the local rulers using the property of the victims, thus the sect managed to survive for a long time. When the British arrived in India, they were not willing to tolerate the activities of the sect, so they chased its members every place, until the beginning of the 19th century when they managed to destroy it altogether. Therefore, the connection between religion and terrorism is ancient and is not a unique phenomenon of these days. Although, as we shall see below, several developments have happened in the last decades regarding the degree of religious influence on terrorism and on the status of religious terrorist organizations in the global terrorist arena.

The donkey, the rabbi and the bible

Since time immemorial religion and violence have been interrelated. Thus, the use of terrorism is not an outlier and not a "mutation" of religion. The connection between religion and violence appears in many religions, and yet a religion is not necessarily the cause of conflicts. Economic, social and geo-strategic factors also play an important role in explaining the connection between religion and terrorism. Generally, in times of tension and despair, secular political conflicts take on a religious turn and the conflict focuses on matters of sanctity and faith.[79]

This claim is expressed in the amusing story of a Jew who comes to a town in Eastern Europe on a donkey. He asks the first man he meets to what can he tie his donkey? The man told him he should go and ask the rabbi. The Jew asks him: "Why the rabbi? What is the matter with the rabbi here?" The man told him: "You want to tie the donkey to something, and the rabbi knows how to tie anything to the bible." Often, after Sabbath sermons in the synagogue, the preacher manages to tie actual events to the same week's reading in the bible. Every incident that occurred - a war, corruption, terrorist attacks, economic crisis, storms, etc. - appeared in the holy text written thousands of years ago.

This phenomenon is not accidental. Religion is a means of interpreting reality, and it helps people understand the world around them. It is a central basis for individual and group identity and a source of moral norms and traditions. Therefore, it plays a central role in conflicts, even in those that are not driven solely by religious reasons. Moreover, people believe in religious interpretation, so they will fight to protect it and believe it will set their guidelines of modus operandi permitted (even killing unarmed civilians). If so, religious institutions may accelerate to violent conflicts, because they may give legitimacy to act violently.[80]

Indeed, an analysis of terrorist attacks from 2001-2009 found that religious terrorism was often caused by a lack of religious freedom. Countries in which freedom of religion is granted, are relatively protected from terrorism on religious grounds, but states that impose restrictions on religions encourage terrorism on religious grounds.[81] According to other studies, a religion itself is not a source of terrorism, but the problem is the discrimination of religious minority groups which belong to a different religion from the majority. This situation is used to recruit supporters for terrorist organizations.[82] However, only a few studies have found a link between religious oppression and the degree of conflict in society.[83] Therefore, arguments about the relationship between terrorism and discrimination on religious background and marginalization are not solid.

If true, and religion is a source of the potential use of violence in general and terrorism in particular, it raises the question if indeed terrorism in the name of religion is more common in the last decades? If so, what explains the growth of religious terrorism? The connection of religion to political violence has recently been discussed in the research literature and several explanations have been offered. Some of the explanations are given here although they do not focus specifically about using terrorism on religious grounds but in the growth of religious conflicts in general.

The first explanation is the theory of secularization. According to this theory, as education, urbanization, and science evolve, religion is perceived as primitive and takes less space in modern life. Therefore, it also becomes irrelevant to collective activity and to justifying political moves.[84] If this is true, then religion should not be a source of violent conflict in general and specifically of resorting to terrorism. Still, it is difficult to eradicate religious beliefs, as Sam Harris wrote sarcastically: Say to a Christian that his devout wife is cheating on him or frozen yogurt can make a person invisible, and like everyone else he will ask you for proof of his satisfaction only in accordance with the strength of the evidence you provide. Tell him that the book he was holding at his bedside was written by an invisible deity who will punish him with eternal fire if he does not receive all that is written in it, and it does not require any proof.[85] In other words, despite the power of modern beliefs, religiosity is rooted strongly and has a meaningful role for politics, political violence and terrorism.

According to another explanation, the role of religion in social life has not changed over the years, that is, it does not take a more central role than in the past and is not more marginal today. Violent conflicts over religious backgrounds, including the use of terrorism, should therefore remain at a frequency as in the past [86].

Contrary to the previous explanation, the role of religion in violent conflicts, including conflicts where terrorism has been used, is gaining a more important role. Scholars disagree on the point in time when religion began to provoke conflicts. Huntington argued that since the end of the Cold War in 1990 conflicts have been based on cultural identity and are conducted between different cultures. These cultures largely overlap with the major religions of the world.[87] If the predictions of Huntington indeed are correct (he wrote his article in the first half of the 1990s), from the 1990s onwards we would face an intensification of interreligious conflicts in general and conflicts between Islam and the West in particular, including the use of terrorism.

Mark Juergensmeyer wrote about the growth of religious violence, and he believed that over the years religion was a more prominent factor than ever before.[88] Therefore, we can expect that because religion will encourage conflicts, violence in general and the use of terrorism on religious grounds in particular will increase. Indeed, depending on the belief that when religious groups feel there is a threat to their identity and their survival, they turn to terrorism, religion and its institutions serve as a means of recruitment to terrorist organizations, and they see their activity as justified. As Sheik Fadlallah, who was the spiritual leader of Hezbollah, said: "When Islam fights war, it fights like any other power in the world, defends itself to preserve its existence and freedom, is forced to take preventive actions when in danger."[89]

Rapoport believed that ideologies which justify terrorism were operating in waves, rising and fading every few decades. At the end of the 19th century, a wave of anarchist terrorism irrupted, and after World War II socialist and ethno-national terrorism intensified. In the last years of the 1970s or the beginning of the 1980s against the background of the Islamic revolution in Iran, the Soviet invasion of Afghanistan and the war of the Mujahideen, we experienced a wave of religious terrorism that has lasted until the present.[90] Rapoport pointed to the decline of socialist, national and secular terrorism and believed that nowadays the wave of terrorism is different. This is the fourth wave of terrorism, characterized by religions, and mostly Islamic motivated.[91] Indeed, from the 1980s to the present, the scale of religious terrorist activity has increased, and the number of religious terrorist organizations has increased. Therefore, it is not a surprise that in the 1970s religious conflicts were taking up a larger portion of the total of all domestic disputes, and therefore often are referred to as the "religious conflicts wave".[92]

One study examined Rapoport's theory, the "waves theory", and found that in the 37 years that were examined by the study there was an increase of terrorist activity. Also, it was found that anarchist terrorist organizations almost did not exist anymore and that ethno-national terrorist organizations had reduced their activity. The scope of activity of left-wing terrorist organizations increased, but from the 1990s onwards fell considerably, while the number of religious terrorist organizations rose.[93]

Another study examined the prevalence of terrorism, and it appeared that we are living in a period of growth in religious terrorism. This study examined about 1,500 terrorist organizations that carried out transnational terrorist attacks and examined the frequency of terrorist organizations' activity depending on their ideology.[94] It was found that until the second half of the 1980s the most active terrorist organizations were left-wing and nationalist terrorist organizations whose activity rate was twice as high, and sometimes even four times the activity rate of religious terrorist organizations.

However, from the mid-1980s to the 2000s, the frequency of transnational attacks of religious terrorist organizations have increased, while the frequency of attacks by nationalist and left terrorist groups diminished. The gap has narrowed greatly, and it is now stands at only a ratio of about 1.4 in favor of national and left-wing terrorist organizations. Regarding violent conflicts the study found that from the end of the 1970s the rate the conflicts (not just those made in the use of terror) based on the same religion have been raised.[95]

Therefore, religious terrorism is a growing phenomenon that existed in a lesser scope also decades ago, and it increased, both because of the religious factors and politico-economic backgrounds in which the religious terrorist organizations work. Huntington's thesis about the clash of civilizations has been of great interest in public and academic discourse and will be discussed here in detail.

Huntington gives the tone?

Huntington argued that the conflicts in the post-Cold War world would be mostly intercultural conflicts and not economic or ideological ones. There are many reasons: culture is an essential identity base both to the individual and to various civilizations (Western; Confucian; Japanese; Islamic; Hindu; Slavic-Orthodox; Latin-American; and African) and therefore less flexible than political or economic identities. In contrast identities that rely on the nation state are weakening, as the world is "shrinking" due to globalization processes, and encounters with other cultures are becoming more frequent and increasing awareness of differences between cultures. Understanding intercultural differences and weakening identities that rest on the nation-state reinforces identities that rest on civilization. Such an identity serves as a new basis for conflicts in the international system. Strengthening an identity based on civilization occurs also because of the power of the West and its global presence which provokes a backlash against a return to the cultural and identity roots. Huntington thus stood for polarization among the great civilizations of mankind, especially polarization between Western culture and Islam. He believed that the fault lines in world politics are changing and that they no longer stem from ideology but from cultural differences.[96]

Huntington's explanation has been of great interest, and it directly concerns the question of whether religion and Islamic civilization are the source of terrorism. An approach that sees cultural-religious polarization in general and Islam in particular as a cause of terrorism is problematic for several reasons. For one, each culture has its own shades, and it is not made from one piece. Even Islam itself is not made from one piece, and the disputes and differences are large even among Muslims. Moreover, due to the processes of cultural globalization, cultures are often not "free" from external influences, and therefore it is impossible to see them as completely different from each other. Also, many times members of cultures who oppose elements in other cultures adopt parts of their norms and values or use the tools it gives them to promote their own cultural values.[97]

According to Huntington's theory, it is expected that in the post-Cold War the rate of intercultural conflicts will increase, especially the rate of conflicts between Islam and other cultures and between Islam and the West. But, not as expected according to the theory, a deeper look shows that the post-Cold War rate of participation of Muslims in conflicts with intercultural conflicts dropped. Since 1990 it has amounted to 46.5% compared to approximately 50.8% during the Cold War. The rate of Cold War conflicts where Muslims were involved accounted for about 24% of all violent ethnic conflicts (intra-cultural and inter-cultural together), but after the Cold War the share of conflicts where Muslims were involved was about 27% only. Moreover, the rate of incidents of violence resulting from clashes between Western and Islamic culture has not increased.[98] Also most of the conflicts in which Muslims were involved were with other Muslims and not with members of other civilizations.[99] If so, it seems that Muslims are indeed participating in the conflicts after the end of the Cold War, but most of them are intra-religious conflicts within Islamic civilization, and therefore in the opinion of Emanuel Sivan, there is no clash between civilizations but a clash mostly within Islam.[100]

Islam against the West?

The studies presented so far do not examined the analysis of terrorism, but other types of violence such as wars between countries, large-scale political violence, crises that escalate into wars between countries and more.[101] The data below focus on one question: Does the analysis of terrorist attacks indicate a clash of civilizations and especially a clash between Islamic and the Western civilizations? From the end of the Cold War until the beginning of the 2000s the rate of attacks of Islamic terrorist organizations was equal to that of other terrorist organizations, except with one difference: the rate of victims in attacks by Islamic terrorist organization was higher than the rate of victims in attacks of other terrorist organizations.[102] That is, unlike Huntington's claim, the rate of terrorist attacks did not increase in the decade following the end of the war. Eric Jungermaier and Thomas Plumper evaluated the rate of victims of terrorist activities that took place on a cultural background. The table below shows the summary of their findings. It shows the rate of fatalities from transnational terrorist attacks in 1969-2005 sorted by civilizational origin of the attackers and civilizations of the victims. I would like to comment that although their study examined data up to 2005 only, the examination of the data is satisfactory because the examination of the data lasted 16 years after the Cold War, a period long enough to assess the differences between the Cold War period and post-Cold-War period.

Table 3: Number of Deaths from Transnational Terrorism by Civilizations[103]

% From Sum	Total of All Terrorist Attacks	West	Islam	Perpetrators of Terrorist Attacks
14	1304	357	29	Africa
4.5	415	362	0	Hindu
46.3	4307	2509	1396	Islam
3.3	309	184	104	Japanese
11.1	1034	335	3	Latin
4	369	28	22	orthodox

6	560	188	6	Other*
2.9	269	2	0	Chinese
7.9	735	683	34	West
	9302	4648	1594	Sum
		50	17.1	% of World Total

*Other includes Haiti and Ethiopia.

Some interesting findings emerge from the table: It seems that citizens of Western countries are the main victims of transnational terrorism (about 50% of all deaths in the world). A small majority of Westerners were murdered by Muslim terrorists (about 54% of all Western casualties). In addition, perpetrators from Islamic civilization have caused the largest number of deaths in transnational terrorist attacks, and the deaths are not only from the West (about 46% of all deaths in the world). It should be noted that about 88% of Muslim victims are victims of terrorist attacks perpetrated by Muslims!

The statistical analyzes conducted by Neumayer and Plumper confirmed part of Huntington's prediction about an increase in the rate of intercultural violence after the Cold War from 1990 onwards. However, Islamic terrorism against other cultures has not intensified. Terrorism of other civilizations against the West did not intensify either. One finding supported Huntington's prediction: after the Cold War, the rate of Western casualties from Muslim terrorist attacks rose. That is, the struggle of Islamic terrorist organizations against Western countries has intensified to some extent, so the finding is consistent with Huntington's hypothesis.

If intercultural conflicts do not explain these findings, what does it explain? According to the researchers, the real considerations for the terrorist activities are strategic. In other words, terrorists are not driven by considerations of intercultural warfare. They aim to increase terrorist attacks against Western countries and increase the rate of victims of terrorism because Western countries provide economic and military assistance to the terrorists' homeland countries, against which they are fighting.

Al Qaeda is the terrorist organization most identified with the clash of civilizations, but it serves as a good example of the strategic argument. Abdullah Azzam, who was the spiritual mentor of Osama Bin Laden, designed in the mid-1980s the idea of global jihad, an idea that later unified the whole branches in the al-Qaida around the world. According to this concept jihad against Islamic regimes will not work, since in the global age it is not possible to fight them only on a local level. Therefore, jihad is required to be a global struggle. It must strike at the Western economy, the source of the power of the infidel and corrupted Islamic regimes.[104] The purpose of this worldview was to provide an Islamic response to the global era, an era in which American-Western values dominated the world so the threat of Islam needed to be on a global scale.[105]

In the beginning there were deep disagreements between Azzam and Al-Zawahiri, deputy of bin Laden (later, after bin Laden was killed, he succeeded him). Al-Zawahiri believed they should fight the local regimes, "the near enemy," and especially the Egyptian regime.[106] By contrast, in connection with the capture of Azzam, bin Laden said in 1996 that the goal is to expel US forces from the Arabian Peninsula and the holy places, to overthrow the Saudi regime and support the worldwide Islamic Revolution.[107] In 1998, bin Laden and al-Zawahiri issued a joint statement reflecting a fundamental change in Al-Qaeda's strategy. The main change was an attack on the "the distant enemy", the worldwide alliance of Crusaders and the Jews, and especially the citizens of the United States.[108]

In 2001, Al-Zawahiri published the book "Knights Under the Prophet's Flag", which discussed Al-Qaeda's transformation from a local organization to an anti-Western global organization that recognizes the globalism of the "distant enemy", which fights the jihadists: "The struggle for the establishment of the Islamic State cannot be waged at the regional level. It is clear that the Jewish-Crusader alliance, led by the United States, will not allow any Muslim force to reach power in any of the Islamic countries. It will mobilize its power to hit it and remove it from power. Towards that end, it will open a battlefront against it that includes the whole world."[109] In other words, the rate of major terrorist attacks on Western countries is not due to a struggle among civilizations but to strategic considerations, the main one being the support of Western countries for certain governments. For example, the chances of Islamic terrorist organizations attacking Sweden are considerably smaller than the chances of them attacking the United States. Also, the likelihood that terrorists from Saudi Arabia or Egypt will attack the United States is considerably higher than the likelihood that the attackers will come from Malaysia, even though Malaysia is a country with a considerable Muslim majority.

Having examined the role of religion in violent conflicts in general and in the world of terrorism in particular, we will turn to other questions: What are the characteristics of religion that help religious terrorist organizations and do not exist in non-religious terrorist organizations? What are the implications of these religious characteristics for the quality of religious terrorist organizations' activities?

Deadly holiness

Religion is a central part of the human experience, so harming the religion of any group, real or imagined, can lead to a very violent conflict. In a religious conflict, the level of violence will be even higher than in a non-religious conflict, because restrictions on the individual's religion impair his ability to fulfill the purpose of his life and give meaning to his life according to divine commandment, as he sees it.

Indeed, a comprehensive statistical analysis regarding intra-state violent conflicts from 1945 to 2000 showed that religion has influenced the extent and the probability of outbreak of such conflicts. Other factors, however, such as the desire for national self-determination, influenced, even more than religion, the outbreak of violent domestic conflicts. Moreover, resolution of violent conflicts is much harder when religion is part of them. Like the story of a foreign journalist who visits the Western Wall in Jerusalem. She was very curious about what occurs in that holy place. She approached an elderly Jew that just finished praying by the Western Wall and he folds his prayer shawl off. She walked to him and asked: "How often do you pray here,"? And the Jew answered her: "Every day for 40 years." "And what for do you pray?" asks the journalist. The Jew answers her: "I pray that the Jews and the Palestinians will live in peace together." The journalist was amazed and said to him: "Great! How is your feeling after 40 years of praying for peace at the Western Wall?" The Jew replies to her: "Well, after 40 years of praying for peace, I feel like I am speaking to a wall."

As with religious conflicts, religious terrorism has unique characteristics that distinguish it from non-religious terrorism.[110] Religion is a powerful source of legitimacy for many things, including the killing of civilians, because it represents sacred commandments, based on the scriptures.[111] Therefore, religion, and especially its strict interpretations, makes it possible to justify terrorist attacks. Moreover, when religious groups use terrorism, religion and terrorism reinforce the legitimacy of each other.[112] Religious issues outweigh the agenda of the day in the public and for which the successful terrorist attacks may strengthen the status of religious in society.[113]

According to an economic theory known as "goods club", public services, such as a subscription to the pool or gym, remain limited to a specific group. The Goods Club is in the middle between public goods and private goods, that is, the rate of beneficiaries is greater than the rate of beneficiaries of private property, but smaller than the rate of beneficiaries of goods open to the public. One of the explanations for the success of religious terrorist organizations in recruiting activists and preserving their power rests on this theory: Religious terrorist organizations serve their operatives as a "goods club". Religious organizations often provide the public that supports them with goods that others do not receive, especially in places where the state fails to provide basic services or where the economy is in a poor condition. The goods are not accessible to everyone but only to sympathizers and potential supporters. For example, Hamas compensates the families of the dead who perpetrated terror attacks on behalf of the organization and the families of the activists in prison. In addition, it takes care of the needy people and nurtures a network of institutions that provide cheap and accessible education and medical treatment.

How do religious organizations manage to do this? On the one hand the restrictions regarding religion alienate those who do not really support the organization, but just want to enjoy what the organization has to offer. On the other hand, keeping the religious restrictions makes a distinction between members of the religious club and the rest of the population. That is strengthened by the desire to participate among those who remain in the group. In this way, religious terrorist organizations succeed in recruiting activists to their ranks, maintaining their resilience and support over time and strengthen the willingness to sacrifice among their comrades.[114]

So far, we have discussed the benefits of religion in recruiting activists to terrorist organizations. However, one of the special characteristics of religious terrorist organizations is their lethality. One of the studies examined the relationship between the degree of lethality of terrorist organizations in the years 1970-2012 and their religiosity. A clear connection was found between the lethality of the terrorist organizations and the rate of attacks they carried out and the religious elements in the ideology of the organization.[115] Another study, which examined terrorist attacks in which killed more than 100 people, found that about 56% of the deaths in those terrorist attacks were killed by religious terrorist organizations. All the rest of the terrorist organizations (left, right, ethno-national, ethno-national-religious and others) were responsible for less than half of all deaths. Even if we take out the number of September 11th casualties, it was found that religious terrorist organizations were responsible for a higher number of fatalities than terrorist organization with other ideologies.[116]

However, the picture seems to be more complex. One of the studies examined the fatalities of terrorist organizations in the years 1968-2004 and found that through 1986 the non-religious organizations were more lethal than the religious ones and in 1987 religious terrorist organizations became more lethal. Each year after, they caused a higher death rate than terrorist organizations with different ideologies.[117] The following graph shows data up to 2005. Studies that analyzed data in subsequent years also had similar conclusion.

Figure 2: Average Number of Victims of Terrorist Attacks by Type of Ideology of Terrorist Organizations 1968-2005

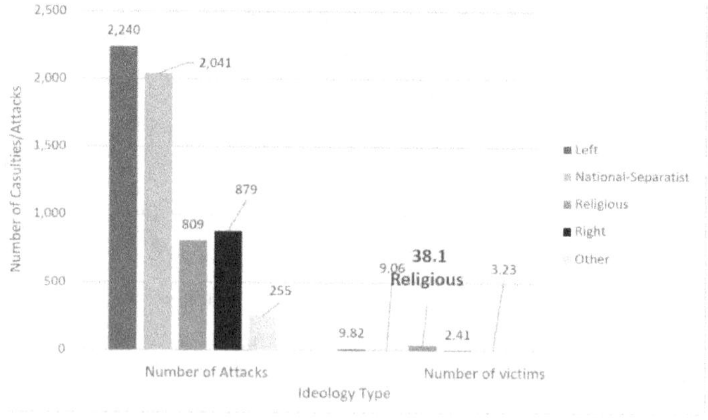

Left: Anarchists, Anti-Globalization, Communists, Socialists and Environmental Right: Racists, Right-wing Conservatives and Right-wing Reactionaries Other: Lacking political affiliation and having criminal motives.

The data shown in the graph can be illustrated by the story of the combined terrorist attack on the Madrid railway system on March 11, 2004. The heated political debate back then revolved around the question of who carried out the attack and what its political consequences might be? The combined terrorist attack on the trains in Madrid killed 200 person and injured 2,000 in different locations, almost at the same time. It was one of the deadliest terrorist attacks on European soil and the deadliest attack in Spain. The attack took place three days before the Spanish elections, and soon the question of the identity of the perpetrators was the burning question of the election campaign. The two competing parties, the Socialist Workers Party and the Party of the People, charged each other with the responsibility of the attacks. The leadership of the ruling party declared ETA (Basque separatist terrorist organization), that is not religious organization, but fights for the establishment of a Basque state, committed the attack, while the party opposing argued that others carried out the attack.

The question of the identity of the perpetrators was essential, because Spain participated in the multinational force in Iraq. The assumption was that if the perpetrators of the attacks were Muslims, it meant that the ruling party was the one that brought the terrorist attacks on the Spaniards due to sending armed forces to Iraq. Alternatively, if the perpetrators of the attacks are indeed Basques, there was no connection to the foreign policy of the ruling government. Aznar, the leader of the People's Party, wanted to keep his seat, and he declared that the ETA organization had carried out the terrorist attacks. The organization was quick to announce through the Spanish media that it denied any connection to the terrorist attacks. This is not surprising, since terrorist attacks with such a high number of casualties could have eroded the organization's legitimacy. Even its supporters were likely to rebel against it and the Spanish authorities would have been given the legitimacy to conduct a harsh campaign against ETA. At the same time, evidence was found that the ETA was not the one who carried out the terrorist attacks, and this angered the voters. They protested the failed attempt to deceive the public and hide the suspicion that these were Muslim terrorists. Three days later in the election Prime Minister Aznar was defeated.

Why in the first place was it reasonable to belief that the Basque organization did not carry out the terrorist attacks? Some characteristics in these attacks did not match its routine pattern of action: Many times, the organization hit specific people, meaning a distinct attack. Moreover, the organization used to give advance notice before detonating explosive devices so that civilians could evacuate the place, and so almost all of the organization's terrorist attacks ended in a very low number of casualties (except for one exceptional attack in which 21 people were killed), but the terrorist attack in Madrid carried out without any prior warning, conducted in several centers, with the intention of killing as many people as possible. The scale of the damage was enormous, and the number of fatalities was much higher than the number of fatalities inflicted by ETA in its entire history. Also, the attack was random and not to a specific person. This form of action was reminiscent of Al Qaeda's known operations. Indeed, after a lengthy investigation, the Spanish authorities concluded that it was Muslims of North African descent who carried out the attack (inspired by Al-Qaeda but not under its direct instruction).

This case is an example of the difference between religious and non-religious terrorist organizations. ETA is not a religious organization, but a national separatist one, while the perpetrators of the attack were Muslims who were actively inspired by a religious terrorist organization. The difference in the death toll matched Al-Qaeda's pattern of action rather than the Basque organization.

Figure 2 also shows the huge difference in the average casualty rate of attack between national-separatist organizations (9.06) and religious terrorist organizations (38.1). Why do religious terrorist organizations differ from terrorist groups who are not religious when it comes to the rate of fatalities? Several factors may explain the phenomenon. One is the desire of terrorists to show that they maintain the dignity of their culture.

This desire is intensified when they act against foreign rivals who they perceive harm their way of life. That conception promotes total alienation toward the enemy, eliminating any element of identification with them, so the barrier to mass killing is removed.[118] Secular terrorist organizations strive to evoke empathy for their own purposes, but religious terrorist organizations do not aspire to have broad legitimacy for the terrorist attacks they perform. They expect spiritual retribution; in their view, the terrorist attack is a purifying action, regardless of the political purpose. Because of such views, they release all restraint in carrying out terrorist attacks and cause many victims.[119] Moreover, unlike secular terrorist organizations that work against some government, religious terrorist organizations often wage war against other societies or cultures, and they strive for terrorist attacks to be particularly lethal.[120] Another explanation is that zealots do not have moral constraints, because the violence they use is justified in relation to their religious belief and the support of their religious community.[121]

Hoffman argues that secular terrorist organizations differ much from religious terrorist organizations in their values, morals and legitimacy. For the religious terrorist, violence is a sacred, supreme duty, a kind of religious commandment. The religious terrorist believes in the existence of another dimension, beyond this world, and therefore the perpetrators of religious terrorism are not affected by political and moral restrictions that apply to other terrorists. Some secular terrorist organizations consider indiscriminate killing an act that is unworthy and immoral, while religious terrorist organizations justify such killing and believe it is necessary to achieve their goals.[122]

Hoffman's remarks suggest that religious terrorists are aspiring to destroy very large groups of enemies. The desire to destroy rests on religious arguments, so religious terrorists believe that such actions are not only moral but also necessary in the overall religious struggle. Anyone who does not belong to their religious group is made a target for terrorist attacks. Moreover, religious terrorist organizations see themselves outside the social system and strive for a new socio-political order. Hence, they believe they can use more destructive violence than non-religious terrorist organizations.

Religious terrorist organizations are particularly dangerous to international security: they see their struggle as between the forces of light and the forces of darkness, and in their view, this allows them to harm anyone who does not belong to their group. As well, religious terrorists use violence to appease a divine entity, so they are not affected by the reaction of their supporters. They are not committed to secular values and even feel alienated from the social environment. Hence, many times they do not try to fix the socio-political system but to replace it.[123]

If these arguments are true, then the religious terrorist organizations should be more violent because they are religious.

What do the data say about it? Indeed, as we have seen in Figure 2, religious terrorist organizations are more deadly on average, but the picture is more complex. According to the findings, not only religion is a factor in severe terrorist attacks but there are also other factors, such as organizational characteristics.[124] Therefore, on the one hand, there is the common claim that religious organizations which seek to fulfill a religious ideology are responsible for attacks with the most lethal rates.[125] ISIS is an example of such a terrorist organization of a pure religious ideology. By the end of 2016, ISIS (including ISIS in Iraq and Syria) had killed more than 30,000 people in 5,194 terrorist attacks. Terrorist organizations that are active many years more than ISIS have not killed so many people. This organization became particularly lethal as it left Iraq and began operations in Syria. On the other hand, it seems that terrorist organizations which have mixed religious and national ideology are more violent than terrorist organizations with pure religious ideology.[126]

Studies on violent conflicts (not necessarily terrorism) have found that the intensity of conflicts among various religious groups is higher than the intensity of other conflicts. However, the connection between religious conflicts and the intensity of the conflict disappears when the researchers considered the question of whether religion was relevant to the conflict, since conflicts among groups which belong to several religions do not necessarily revolve around religious values. Moreover, they found no difference between different religions in the degree of the intensity of the conflict in which they were involved.[127]

All in all, the picture is more complex, and the claim that religion causes a high death rate in terrorist attacks is too simplistic. Indeed, terrorist organizations with a religious ideological component are more violent, but as will be explained later, that a religious terrorist organization is likely to be lethal depends on the design of the religious idea (local or global), the degree of influence of religion on the organization's set of values and characteristics and other organizational characters.

What about the impact of religion on suicide terrorism? Some scholars argue that suicide terrorism stems from the nature of Islam or the conditions prevailing in the Muslim world.[128] However, other researchers point to other factors, such as occupation, oppression, ethnic divisions or competition among terrorist organizations.[129] Today, it is accepted view among scholars that religion affects political violence through the recruitment of activists to terrorist organizations, but its influence is less than other, non-religious motives.[130]

Many terrorist organizations have committed suicide attacks: religious terrorist organizations of all religions - Muslims (Shiites and Sunnis), Christians, Hindus, Sikhs - and secular terrorist organizations.[131] Herewith, the perception prevalent is that a dispute taking place through suicide terrorism is necessarily an Islamic one.[132] Martyrdom in the sense of heroic death for the sake of the group is not a purely religious idea. Secular terrorist organizations, such as the PKK, contribute significantly to the global rate of suicide terrorist attacks.[133] However, it turns out that the religiosity of terrorist organizations is related to the considerably higher rate of deaths in terrorist suicide attacks, other characteristics of the organization, such as the structure of the organization (hierarchic or networked), should also be considered.

From an analysis of the data of 2,200 suicide attacks in 1980-2006 it was found that religious terrorist organizations carried out 841 attacks. Even if we omit some 1,180 attacks where it is not known what organizations committed them, religious terrorist organizations carried out about 82% of all attacks. The average of fatalities in suicide terrorist attacks perpetrated by non-religious terrorist organizations was 8 deaths, while the average number of those killed in suicide attacks committed by religious terrorist organizations were about 12 deaths - in that group the fundamentalists have caused an average number of almost 24 deaths per suicide attack. A significant positive statistical relationship was also found between religious ideology and the number of people killed in suicide attacks.[134] If so, it seems that although many organizations carry out suicide attacks, a considerable portion of the terrorist organizations that carry out suicide attacks are religious terrorist organizations.

Is Islam a root cause of terrorism?

About two months after the terrorist attacks in the United States in September 2001, a survey was conducted among American citizens. 61% of them agreed that the United States should support democracy and economic growth in Muslim countries. At the same time, they believed that religious extremism was the main cause of transnational terrorism.[135] These positions indicate the perception that the religion of Islam was a major source of terrorism. In academia, too, the perception may be heard that violence and terrorism are an integral part of the religion of Islam.[136] Such perceptions rest on the assumption that in Islam there is no separation between religion and politics and unlike Christianity, Islam has never abandoned the idea of religious war against infidels (the term jihad also includes nonviolent aspects, such as preaching or moral confrontation). Indeed, many extremist religions sought to transform their environment to their religion. Moreover, religious terrorism is more prevalent among Muslims than among believers of other religions. Herewith, most of the Muslims do not turn to the path of terrorism.[137] Also it would not be correct to claim that terrorism has always been a tool that helped Muslims in their war. All that can be said is that many Muslims carry out terrorist attacks. Also, we can say that certain currents in Islam justify the extensive use in terrorism in recent decades and the rate of participation of Islamic terrorist organizations worldwide increased considerably. A key component of religious terrorism in general and Islamic jihad in particular is the restoration of Islamic honor and the restoration of the status of Islam in the contemporary world order.[138] In interviews conducted by Jessica Stern with religious active terrorists, she reported that the activists were striving to purge the current world from injustice and hoping to make it a better place. In their view, there is no room for the views of others since the population they represent is humiliated, discriminated and powerless. Any act of terrorism will be justified in their eyes both in terms of political and moral aspects.[139]

Another argument is that the Muslim world is particularly prone to terrorism due to economic underdevelopment and the oppression of dictatorships, hence the reference to terrorism not being a built-in component of religion itself. Scott Atran argued that the ideology of Islam is not the main cause of terrorism today in general and suicide terrorism in particular, at least no more than other factors.[140] Moreover, in his opinion, fundamentalist religiosity has intensified all over the world, not only among Muslims, and that the most fundamentalist Muslims do not perpetrate terrorist attacks.

There are also conspiracy claims whereby after the breakup of the communist bloc the claims about connection between terrorism and Islam stem from the need of Western countries to create an external enemy.[141] Still, how do we explain the relatively high proportion of participation in terrorism among countries whose population is Muslim? How do we explain the high prevalence of Islam-inspired terrorism?142 To answer these questions we must examine the empirical analyses.143

Islam against all the rest?

As mentioned, according to a series of studies conducted in the early 2000s, religion was a major factor in encouraging terrorism.[144] According to Hoffman, although the rate of attacks by religious terrorist organizations out of all terrorist attacks in the 1980s was relatively low, the rate of casualties in terrorist attacks by Muslim terrorist organizations was particularly high, even more than the rate of casualties from other religious terrorist organizations.[145] In his opinion, Islamic terrorist organizations cause an increase in the lethality of religious terrorist organizations.[146]

However, the findings are not conclusive,[147] so we should carefully review the data. Research conducted by James Piazza analyzing data for the years 1968 to 2005 found that Islamic terrorist organizations were responsible for approximately 94% of terrorist attacks perpetrated by religious terrorist organizations and responsible for 87% of the victims. Non-Islamic terrorist organizations caused 8.7 victims per attack, but Islamic terrorist organizations caused 21 victims per attack.[148] Other studies have also found that Muslim countries have suffered from terrorist attacks more than non-Muslim countries, for example, from suicide terrorism[149]; these differences probably resulted from supporting Islamist ideas, such as Jihad, protecting Islam and martyrdom (istishhad).[150]

If we will deepen the analysis of the data and consider the types of Islamic organizations, it was revealed that in 1968-2005 138 Islamic terrorist organizations were active, which carried out 1,543 attacks, and these attacks claimed the lives of 32,444 victims. Of these attacks, Al-Qaeda and its affiliated organizations carried out 678 attacks and claimed the lives of 24,460 victims. That is a group of organizations that is particularly violent and deadly.[151] It seems that non-Al-Qaeda-affiliated Islamic terrorist organizations are not lethal more than other terrorist organizations.[152]

Terrorist organizations affiliated to Al Qaeda have a global and abstract ideology, while the goals of other Islamic terrorist organizations, such as Hamas, are strategic and defined usually related to a specific territory. They are engaged with the local population and committed to supply the everyday needs of their potential supporters. Global terrorist organizations have broad and ambitious goals, which are driven primarily by ideology, so their attacks do not stem only from military necessities, but mainly for an aspiration and for advertising in the media. As well, universal terrorist organizations represent populations spread in many places in the world. These populations maintain loose ties, based on ideology. Global terrorist organizations directed the messages carried by their attacks to these people. They seek to spread these messages globally to increase the commitment of their potential support groups. Those terrorist organizations are more violent than other terrorist organizations because many attacks that cause many casualties have two main functions: to send a message to supporters and potential enemies that the level of their commitment to their cause is very high[153] and draw the attention of the global media in marketing their messages to the entire world.[154]

Summary

The connection between religion and terrorism is not a new phenomenon. The perception that religion is a factor that encourages terrorism has strengthened since the mid-1980s. Most religious terrorism or Islamic terrorism is not due to a clash of civilizations in general or from a clash with the Western civilization in particular. In fact, the clash is mainly within Islam. Even when Western countries are attacked, the attacks stem from strategic motives, as they are intentional towards specific countries assisting the enemies of terrorist organizations.

Terrorist organizations with a religious ideology cause more casualties than non- religious terrorist organizations. However, other reasons - such as ideology, nationality or how their goals were designed (locally or globally) – also affect their behavior. Most terrorist organizations that carried out suicide attacks were terrorist organizations with a religious ideological component, and they also caused the largest death rates relative to the other organizations.

In general, not all Muslims are terrorists and not all terrorists are Muslims. The rate of Islamic terrorist organizations is very high nowadays and has risen greatly since the end of 1980s. Moreover, the religion of Islam serves as a justification for terrorist attacks. Still, today non-Islamic terrorist organizations are operating,

and in the past, they were the vast majority in the world
of terrorism.

"We Love Death More Than Our Enemies Love Life"

In Operation Protective Edge in 2014, Israel fought against Hamas and Palestinian Islamic Jihad in the Gaza Strip. The war was led by Hamas, which ruled Gaza and launched rockets on Israeli populated areas long before Israel launched the operation.

Mohammed Deif is the military leader of Hamas who Israel tried many times to assassinate (he was injured several times in the assassination attempts, became disabled but stayed alive and remained active). During the operation, Deif taped a message to the Israelis: "You [Israelis] are fighting today the soldiers of god, who love the death for the sake of Allah as you love life, and [they] compete for martyrdom [sacrifice for the sake of god] as you run from death."[155]

Mohammad Deif, commander of the Brigades Izz a-Din al-Qassam — the military wing of Hamas — was not the first to send such a message. Of course, his statement was made as a piece of psychological warfare, and his message was that the members of Hamas adhered to their cause. They were not afraid to make suicide attacks and did not shy away from death in the war against Israel. Therefore, if Israel fought Hamas, it could suffer many casualties.

This statement rests on the value of sacrifice and suicide for God, a tactic used by Hamas in its struggle against Israel. This chapter will discuss this phenomenon - suicide terrorist attacks. The history of suicide terrorism will be discussed and statistical data about the phenomenon examined. The causes of the phenomenon and whether it is possible to cope with suicide attacks are also looked at.

A suicide attack is an act of political violence where the plan is to commit suicide intentionally during the attack.[156] Suicide terrorism is not a new method at all. A prominent example is the Order of the Hashashin, whose operatives were Ismailis - Nazari. This sect was active from the 11th century through to the 13th century, and its members carried out assassinations. Some researchers claim that these were suicides, because usually their victims were leaders surrounded by guards, and the attackers used knives to assassinate them. Such a course of action almost certainly ensured that the attackers died and shows that the attackers probably sought to perform an act of self-sacrifice.

Another example is Muslim communities in Asia. They lived in southwestern India, northern Sumatra in Indonesia, and Mindanao and Solo in the Philippines in the period from the 18th to the early 20th century. They carried out suicide attacks in these areas for the sake of jihad (holy war) against the colonialist Europeans.[157]

Suicide attacks are not unique to any religion or culture. At the end of the 19th century, Russian anarchists used explosive devices. Sometimes, to ensure the success of the mission, they remained close to the target so that their suicide was conscious and intentional in advance.

Survivors, too, refused to be pardoned and were executed.[158]

In the past, to ensure harm to the enemy, the terrorists had to carry out a suicide attack. However, with developing arms and materials for explosives the need for suicide missions have decreased, since there is no need any more to sacrifice the attacker to make sure a bomb detonates. It can be activated remotely, etc.

However, the readiness to self-sacrifice has not diminished, and the proof is that suicide bombings resumed and intensified in the early 1980s. The first suicide bombing took place in 1981 against the Iraqi embassy. About a year and a half later another attack was carried out, this time against the United States embassy in Beirut. Many people mistakenly believe that the suicide attack on the Marine base in Beirut in October 1983 was the first suicide terrorist attack. However, this attack was still important, because it was a source of inspiration for the murderous suicide bombing of the Tamil tigers in Sri Lanka over the 1980s and 1990s.

What are the benefits of suicide attacks?

Zion Square in Jerusalem city center was almost empty of people, and the only ones seen on the city streets were security forces. On my way to the sidewalk, I got checked twice. This was the time of the Passover holiday and in normal times, the city center is crowded - Jews on their way to the Western Wall, people filling the hotels, cafe and restaurants or attending events on the streets of the city. Where was everyone?

At the Park Hotel, a few days earlier, during the Passover Seder, one of the most severe suicide attacks Israel have ever known happened. Soon after, the IDF launched operation "Defensive Shield." Fear ruled the streets - the impact of terrorist bombers was clear, and it was amazing for those who are used to seeing masses of people on weekdays in this area of the city.

Some benefits of suicide terrorist attacks are: the cost of operation is relatively small and uncomplicated compared to the abduction of hostages or compared to an operation that requires early planning of escape routes and hiding places. Suicide attacks increase the rate of casualties since the suicide bomber can ensure that once the explosion is executed it will cause the largest possible damage. A suicide bomber cannot be investigated, so the potential intelligence damage to the terrorist organization is minimal. Such damage can only happen if the suicide bomber did not ultimately carry out the attack or (rarely) survive it. Moreover, suicide attacks have tremendous impact on the public, because people feel that they are helpless and cannot cope with the determination of the terrorists and their readiness to die.[159]

The rate of average fatalities in suicide attacks (10.47) is higher significantly from the average of those killed in non-suicide terrorist attacks (2.09). Also, the rate of the average number of wounded in suicide attacks (22.64) is higher than the average number wounded in non-suicide attacks (2.54).[160] Moreover, suicide terrorist attacks and bombings attract attention in the media and gain wider publicity than other terrorist attacks. Suicide attacks have a psychological impact that is visible, and through that terrorist organizations aim to achieve concessions from their enemy.[161]

Another advantage of suicide attacks is the symbolic value of martyrdom for a noble cause. This is true not only in Islam but also in other cultures and even in secular organizations. The death of a member of the group reinforces the adherence to the goal and its legitimacy. The groups exploit the fame of the suicide operation to advance the cause and shape a culture of martyrdom in songs, stories and ceremonies. The suicide bomber becomes a famous role model,[162] and therefore the image of the suicide terrorist becomes a powerful tool in recruiting support, strengthening the cohesion of a group, and having a moral justification for the way the terrorists choose.[163]

A terrorist organization may gain political profits from suicide attacks if it competes with another organization. For example, in the conflict between Israel and the Palestinians, suicide attacks are part of the political competition between several organizations, such as Hamas and Palestinian Islamic Jihad.[164]

Suicide attacks are also a tool in managing politics in front of the potential supporters of the terrorist organizations. A study comparing Hamas to Palestinian Islamic Jihad revealed that suicide bombings were a strategic choice of these organizations. Suicide terrorism has appeared whenever political progress has been signaled, after Hamas and Palestinian Islamic Jihad estimated they would be marginalized in Palestinian politics. Indeed, several Palestinian opinion polls have shown support for suicide bombings, especially after the collapse of the political process. Before the year 1996, about 30% of the Palestinian public supported suicide terrorist attacks, and in 2000 the support rose to about 65% and in 2002 soared to nearly 70% support. Arafat, seeing many people start to support Islamic organizations, also began to support terrorist Palestinian attacks.[165] In 2007 polls, the Palestinians continued to support suicide bombings. Similar findings were also found in a survey conducted by PEW in 2013 in 10 Muslim nations and the territories of the Palestinian Authority, where it was found that Palestinians supported suicide attacks more than others (62% responded justified suicide attacks).[166]

The intensification of suicide terrorism

From 1982 until the year 2016 there were 5,430 suicide terrorist attacks around the world - 55,022 people were killed and 135,357 injured. The suicide bombings took place in 54 countries, including Afghanistan, Israel, Syria, Lebanon, Turkey, Iraq, Sri Lanka, the United States, Britain and Morocco. Suicide attacks give civilians a feeling of helplessness and benefit from publicity and wide media coverage. In 1982-2016 there were approximately 170,000 attacks of terrorism around the world and few percentages of them were suicide attacks.

Figure 3: Number of Terrorist Attacks, Fatalities Injures 1982-2019[167]

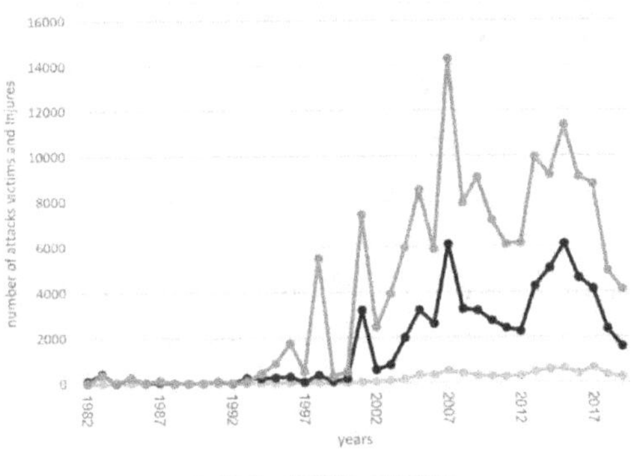

3 shows that in the 1980s the rate of suicide attacks, the rate of deaths and the rate of injuries were relatively low compared to subsequent years. In most of the 1980s, the number of suicide attacks was single-digit, while from the mid-1990s there was a large jump in the rate of suicide attacks: in the years 1994-2003, there were 92-99 suicide attacks per year. For most of the years, their number was in the double-digits. In 2004 the number of terrorist attacks crossed the threshold of the 100 and came to 175 attacks, and since then up until today the number of attacks and suicide attacks is some hundreds every year. The peak year was 2014 with 596 suicide attacks. More than 60% of suicide attacks in the world (in the years 1982-2019) occurred in the last decade. A similar upward trend also emerged at the rate of fatalities and injuries from suicide attacks (Figure 3). Here, too, since the 1980s, there was an increase in the rate of fatalities each year, from a few tens to hundreds in the mid-1990s, and then from 2004 until the year 2019, almost every year, the death toll has stood at several thousand, with the peak year 2015 when 6,117 were killed. Also, the number of wounded grew annually, the peak was in 2007 (14,295), but in the last years, since 2016, there is a decrease in the number of suicide terrorist attacks and the numbers of victims and injuries.[168]

Why has the rate of suicide attacks increased since the 1980s? There is a perception that suicide terrorists are people with a mental disorder, this will be discussed later. Here we only note the problems of mental health of suicide terrorists cannot explain the dramatic increase in the number of suicide attacks in the world, because there is no reason to apply a dramatic increase in the rate of persons under pathological mental conditions.

The explanation of the dramatic increase in the rate of suicide attacks may therefore lie in the network structure of terrorist organizations: the terrorist networks around the world have designed a system that easily allows continuation and persistence of suicide attacks. According to that explanation, the rate of suicide attacks stems from the branched connections within the terror networks, as such attacks are carried out much more easily than before and the information on how to make them distributed much more easily. Another explanation is the element of imitation. Terrorist organizations can easily copy and design the attacks to their unique conditions. It's like a fashion that briefly attracts many people.[169]

Suicide terrorism from the Salafi school (a steam in Islam that wants to renew the days of Islam as in the glory days of the Prophet Muhammad) of terrorist organizations promoted a new pattern of suicide terrorism, which led to the globalization of martyrdom. Unlike the pattern of the past activity of local groups (Tamils, Palestinians and Kurds), today suicide terrorism is less rooted in the local-national context. The growth of Al-Qaeda - an organization belonging to the Salafi school in Islam - is a major factor in the rise in the number of terrorist organizations carrying out suicide bombings and the number of deaths due to suicide missions. This is joined by the ideology of the Salafi jihad, which encourages suicide attacks in the name of God and for the Muslim community as a whole (the "Ummah").

Al-Qaeda sees suicide attacks as a main tactic and was able to make itself a global entity for several reasons: the spread of the Mujahideen warriors (veterans of the Afghanistan War in the 1980s), the global Islamic ideology and the conscious decision to fight the Western countries ("The Far Enemy").[170]

Osama bin Laden, the founder of Al-Qaeda and its former leader, adopted the religious justification for suicide bombings. To spread the idea of Istishhad (the sacrifice for God), his organization used the story of Khaled Ibn al-Walid. In the year 637 in al-Qadisiyyah the Muslim army of Ibn Al-Walid was inferior numerically to the army of the Persians/Sassanians (120,000 soldiers in front of 300,000 Persian soldiers). He sent to the commander of the Persian force a message in these words: "islamu tislamu", which means "if being Islamized, you will have peace." He added: "But if you do not agree, I come to you with my people who love death as you love life." This story became a groundbreaking story in the Islamic historiography, and it was used by Al-Qaeda, for psychological warfare and for the dissemination of the idea of the istishhad to other terrorist organizations as well.[171]

In this context, Al-Qaeda has been a key factor for several reasons: One, it is a networked organization - networks of networks operating in many countries around the world. Sometimes the connection between them is loose or just exists by the very identification with the ideology and practice of the organization. Moreover, the organization's goal is to spread suicide terrorism in as many Islamic organizations as possible. The organization's propaganda emphasizes the activists' commitment to the goal and their determination to commit suicide missions, which intensified the organization's impact on populations around the world that potentially would be supporters of Al-Qaeda. Therefore, many in the world see the organization as a role model. It should be noted that Al-Qaeda (and Da'as/ISIS which split from it) succeeded among other things due to the use of the mass communication media, including the Internet.[172]

Is occupation the cause of suicide terror attacks?

Over the years, researchers have tried to understand why in some of the countries in which terrorism was used, suicide attacks were also used, while in others the use of terrorism was not accompanied by suicide attacks. In other words: why did some terrorist organizations commit suicide attacks while others did not?

Afghanistan, and even more so Iraq, has suffered the highest rate of suicide attacks, and this rate is considerably higher than in other countries. Among the top 10 countries which suffered from suicides attacks Iraq is number one by far more than the countries which are rated in places 3-10 altogether (Pakistan, India, Syria, Yemen, Nigeria, Sri Lanka, Russia, and Israel). On the other hand, note that in most countries of the world no suicide attacks have occurred at all, and in most countries where suicide attacks have taken place, the rate of suicide attacks has been considerably lower than the rate of the top 10 countries.

The list of the 10 countries that suffered the highest rate of suicide terrorism includes Iraq, Afghanistan, Israel, the United States, Sri Lanka, Russia and Lebanon. These are countries controlled by a foreign entity or they are controlling (or have recently ruled) territory that is not part of their sovereign jurisdiction. Some of them are countries where the terrorist organization is separatist and seeks to break away from them. One of the most prevalent explanations in the literature on suicide terrorism is that of Robert Pape. He claims that suicide terrorism is primarily a response to foreign occupation.[173] Therefore, he argued that while religion is somewhat related to suicide terrorism, this phenomenon is primarily an extreme national liberation strategy. This strategy is used against democracies that have sent their military forces to control the territory which the terrorist organizations see as their homeland.[174]

Indeed, from the 1980s to 2013 about half of suicide bombings (1,774 attacks) were carried out against security forces, not against unarmed civilians.[175] In other words, many times terrorist organizations directed their suicide attacks against military targets, which may hint at their ambition to fight a foreign occupier. However, in his study Pape examined terrorist organizations that not only harmed foreign armies, but also attacked the military units of the government of the country, so this figure still does not confirm his claim that suicide attacks are aimed only at foreign occupations.

Pape believes that suicide terrorism stems from a weighting of several factors: strategic calculation, social support, and personal motivation. In his opinion, the main factor is the strategic calculation - forcing the political goals of the terrorist organization on the other side. Almost all suicide attacks are part of a broader campaign; they are not random. Organizations, rather than extremist individuals, carry them out to achieve rational political goals. These goals are essentially national and not religious (undoubtedly, not Islamic ones). Most terrorist organizations that committed suicide terrorist attacks from the 8th century to the 20th onwards - including Hezbollah, the Tamil Tigers, and the PKK - sought to influence the power of occupation of a foreign country (as they saw it). Moreover, in the last few decades most of the states that terrorist organizations have directed suicide attacks against were democracies. According to Pape, democratic countries are more vulnerable to coercion.

If we take a few examples from Pape, we can see certainly the Palestinian-Israeli conflict - with Hamas, Palestinian Islamic Jihad and Fatah - and the war with Hezbollah in southern Lebanon. Israel is a democratic state; Palestinians see the Gaza strip, Judea and Samaria controlled by Israel as an occupying force and, among other things, have used suicide terrorist attacks against it. The case of Hezbollah is also relevant because most of the Lebanese saw the Israeli presence as an occupation of Lebanon and Hezbollah acts against it through suicide bombings. In the beginning of the 1980s Hezbollah saw the international forces as foreign intervention in Lebanon and attacked them and specifically American targets using suicide bombers. Of course, there are other cases in the world that also fit the definition of Pape, such as the suicide bombings in Iraq after the US invasion. The United States is a democratic state, and most Iraqis saw the US as unwanted occupier.

Pape believed that the success of suicide terrorism was the reason for its flourishing in recent decades. It has become a viable tactic in the eyes of terrorist organizations. Of course, for this tactic to be a method of action, the terrorist organization needs the support of the community, in whose name it commits suicide attacks. This requires a great distance from the opposite side, meaning that the enemy undergoes a process of demonization, and a justification for suicide - an act that is usually perceived as taboo - is given.

Not at all cases of occupation in history also brought suicide attacks. Pape's thesis has received much criticism, for example from Sarah Wade and Dan Reiter.[176] Wade and Reiter have not been able to prove Pape's claims, because they did not find a connection between the type of regime and the rate of suicide attacks. Even Piazza did not find any empirical support for the claim that suicide attacks are directed more against democracies that occupy foreign countries. Piazza found that foreign occupation and religious diversity were linked to suicide terrorism. Like Wade and Reiter, Piazza also found that democracies do not suffer from suicide terrorism more than other regimes. However, an examination of the countries of origin of suicide bombers has revealed that terrorists from non-democratic countries tend to carry out suicide attacks more than terrorists from democracies.[177] Moreover, in the 1990s, and even more so in the 2000s, non-national religious terrorist organizations — such as Al-Qaeda and its affiliates — seemed to be responsible for carrying out many suicide bombings. Most of the terrorist attacks were carried out by religious terrorist organizations, and many of the suicide attacks were not directed against the occupying force but against other groups in the local population in the "occupied country". Moreover, terrorist attacks have sometimes been waged against domestic governments, such as in Sri Lanka and Turkey. Furthermore, in certain conflicts some of the perpetrators of suicide attacks came from foreign countries and had foreign citizenship.[178] Meaning, they were not rebels who fought against an occupying regime, but foreigners who intervened in the conflict against another regime. If so, all in all, Pape's claim does not seem to stand the empirical test.

'He was crazy,' said a sophisticated politician

"He was crazy," said a sophisticated politician.
 "Dozens of people were killed," the TV announcer concluded.
"Hopefully we will have quiet evening, now to the commercials".

These three lines are taken from the Mashina band's song: "Goodbye Youth Hello Love." The perception represented in them is that the mass killer who commits suicide intentionally must be insane. After all, a normal man would not commit suicide, of course not for the murder of people. Sometimes the impression created in the media is that the terrorist bomber is someone evil with murderous tendencies, frustrated, not incompetent, a person who grows up in an environment of poverty, ignorant or an anarchist. It seems, therefore, that there is seemingly no hope of eradicating the roots of suicide terrorism.[179]

However, unlike this assumption, it seems that usually suicide terrorists are within the range of the social-psychological norm. Although in some cases turned, it is easier to become a terrorist and commit suicide operations because of their socio-economic background, personal depression, post-trauma or mental illness, but it might be that these people had suicidal inclinations from the beginning.[180]

The perpetrators of suicide attacks may be affected by a group's psychosocial aspects, such as the erasing of personal interests in favor of the interests of the group, identification with the group, social cohesion, obedience to the norms of the group and hostility towards foreign groups - all these increase the chances of committing extreme acts, such as committing a suicide attack.[181] However, we should not conclude that terrorists who commit suicide to kill other people are driven by irrationality or madness. Moreover, as will be discussed below, although many see them as individual extremists, in practice they belong to a terrorist organization, and sending them to their mission is a calculated action.[182]

Waffa Idris worked at the Red Crescent (a medical aid organization similar to the Red Cross and the Red Star of David). On January 27, 2002, Waffa began her suicide mission, dressed in a rescue organization uniform. She hid the explosive device in the ambulance, as she knew that this would be an easy way to get the explosive belt to its destination. Waffa blew herself up in a store in Jerusalem and became the first Palestinian woman to commit a suicide terrorist attack. Many around her believed that the divorce from her cousin - a divorce resulting from her infertility - was the decisive reason for her decision to become a suicide bomber. This was a turning point, and since then Palestinian women's suicide terrorism has become part of the landscape of the Israeli-Palestinian conflict. Waffa was a role model for others, and in the following months intensified the phenomenon of female suicide bombers among Palestinians.[183]

We can learn from Waffa's story that terrorism also requires an understanding of psychological and cultural factors. Herewith, often many motives for terrorist attacks in general such as personal anger and desires for revenge are not different from the motives for suicide terrorist attacks.[184] From the perspective of the suicide bomber himself, he is martyr, his action impresses his social environment, and he will be remembered after his death. This is a fundamental consideration for those who already believe that their life does not have value.[185] Furthermore, children who grow up in culture which glorifies suicide attacks - a culture that provides spiritual, religious or material incentives, such as economic aid for their family and being promised heaven and reverence — may in the future be more easily recruited for suicide attacks.

According to another view, suicide terrorism is a rational tool in the struggle to achieve the goals of the terrorist organization. Suicide attacks are part of an overall terrorist campaign, one of the tactics that terrorist organizations openly choose to achieve a political goal. It is likely that suicide mission volunteers will not be willing to sacrifice themselves if their action does not serve some ideology or strategy.[186] A study that examined the suicide attacks of the Tamils and the suicide attacks of the Palestinians found that in both cases the suicide attacks were mainly a tool to advance the struggle among the active terrorist organizations in the conflict. In both cases they did not stem from the outrageous feelings of the attackers, their despair or frustration.[187] Herewith, the degree of rationality in carrying out suicide attacks is limited, because beyond rational considerations of cost and benefit, many other motives are related to suicide attacks, including personal loss, feelings of humiliation, hatred and commitment to group norms.[188] Before we turn to expand the discussion on suicide attacks and the connection to the mental state of suicide terrorists, we will deal briefly with the question of who is the suicide bomber?

The suicide terrorist

Yasmina Khadra is of the pen name of the Algerian writer Mohammed Moulessehoul, author the book The Attack.[189] The book recounted the story of Amin, a physician from Jenin, who worked at a clinic in Israel. One day his wife carried an explosive belt on her body, while she was pregnant, and committed a suicide attack at a crowded restaurant in Tel Aviv. In the book, Amin the doctor seeks to answer the question: Why? After all, his wife was normative, she had Israeli citizenship, the couple lived in one of Tel Aviv's prestigious neighborhoods, and his wife was on good relations with her Jewish neighbors - why would she carry out a suicide attack on children who went out to celebrate at a restaurant? It is not clear why Shiam, Amin's wife, chose to carry out a suicide attack. Apparently, her profile was not the typical suicide terrorist profile.

Following the terrorist attacks on the United States on September 11, experts made a significant effort to design a profile of suicide bombers. The researchers asked themselves if indeed a terrorist bomber is mad, or has other unique characteristics of any kind? A study of Hamas suicide bombers found that the suicide bombers were men aged 18-28, single and uneducated relative to their surroundings.[190] However, this description was correct for Hamas's suicide bombers during a given period but is not necessarily a valid general profile of suicide bombers. For example, Muhammad Ata - one of the leaders of the 9/11 suicide attacks - was educated and relatively old. So was Shehzad Tanweer, one of the suicide bombers in the London Underground terrorist attacks in July 2005. Tanweer detonated an explosive device on the subway; he himself was killed in the blast and with him six passengers. Tanweer, a member of a family from Pakistan, was born in Yorkshire, and he was not poor or ignorant. His father ran a successful business of foods shipments, and Tanweer had a degree in Sports Sciences from the University of Leeds.[191] Similarly, in the second Intifada (the Second Palestinian terrorist campaign launched in 2000), the suicide bombers were bachelors, married men, women, students and people of high economic status, so it is doubtful whether there is a profile of a suicide bomber.[192] As noted in a report written to the U.S Congress, there is no special psychological trait that characterizes suicide bombers, let alone a unique personality.[193]

Ariel Merri conducted extensive research on suicide bombers. He examined the suicide data of Hezbollah, Amal (Shiite secular Lebanese organization), Hamas and Palestinian Islamic Jihad. He came to the general conclusion that there is no profile, psychological or social, to suicide bombers. It can be learned from his findings that the existence of an escalating conflict makes some people willing to sacrifice themselves for the sake of their goal.[194] Moreover, terrorist organizations are not able to create people who are willing to commit suicide. However, they can locate and mobilize those that have the highest potential to become suicide bombers and strengthen their tendency. As we know, beliefs, religious and national hatred, and feelings of vengeance strengthen willingness to perform suicide attacks.[195]

In the context of the discussion about the characters of the suicide bomber it is important to mention suicide terrorism by women, which has intensified over recent years, and today has an important place in the phenomenon of suicide attacks. In the years 1982-2016, women carried out about 10% of the suicide attacks in which the gender of the suicide terrorist was known. In the 2000s the total number of women suicide bombers was on the rise (but among perpetrators of suicide attacks their share has declined). In the years 1981-1999 women carried 32 attacks and bombings, about 29% of the all the terrorist attacks where the gender of the perpetrator was known; while in the years 2000-2016, they carried out 198 suicide attacks, which is about 8% of the total number of attacks in which the terrorist's gender was known. Moreover, the average number of fatalities in suicide attacks carried out by women was higher than the average number of fatalities in suicide attacks that were carried out by men.[196]

Boko Haram, al-Shabab, the Taliban, Hamas, and the Tamil Tigers – these are all organizations that sent women to carry out suicide missions. Additionally, groups that before did not send women to carry out suicide attacks, due to social and religious causes, have started to do so. Researchers present two reasons for the increase in the number of organizations that send women to carry out suicide attacks: tactical and strategic ones. Recruiting women increases the potential pool of suicide terrorists and women who carry out suicide missions get increased media exposure and have a greater psychological impact on the enemy.[197]

Does poverty cause suicide terrorism?

Like the claims about the connection between poverty, ignorance and terrorism, there are claims about the relations between poverty, ignorance and suicide terrorism. Several academic studies were conducted, including some on the Israeli-Palestinian conflict. One study found that most of the Palestinian suicide bombers had an academic education. Interestingly, during the study period only a small minority of the Palestinian population of similar ages (approximately 13%) had an academic education. It was also found that less than 13% of suicide bombers came from poor families, while at the time of the study, about a third of the Palestinian population lived in relative poverty.[198] Herewith, another study which focused only on Palestinian suicide terrorism, found that the people who carried out suicide missions came from low socioeconomic layers and had fewer family connections. The researchers hypothesized that they felt helplessness and uncertainty regarding the future.[199] Therefore, from the inconsistent findings we learn that the prevailing intuitive perception – that ignorance and poverty cause people to volunteer for suicide attacks - is not solid at all. A more complex and balanced picture of the Palestinian suicide terrorism will be obtained from an understanding of all the causes of suicide attacks. It seems that most of the volunteers for attacks among Palestinians were affected by several factors. However, the weight of each factor and the combination of all the factors together are not clear enough.

Suicide terrorists may be affected by personal and family factors, group pressures, or religious and national motivations. The combination of all the factors is still unclear due to the difficulty of distinguishing between them. For example, it is difficult to distinguish between religious justification for carrying out a suicide attack, which is based on an Islamic religious duty and the belief that the perpetrator will live in heaven, with the knowledge that his family will receive economic profits and social prestige.[200]

According to Assaf Moghadam, terrorist organizations are searching all the time for the next volunteer for a suicide attack. They aim to reach a person with whom the chance to perform the operation successfully is the highest possible. A successful action is an action in which the man who carries out the attack is not caught and is not a waste of resources. The aim of the training and indoctrination is to train the candidate, psychologically and ideologically, to be convinced of the rightness of the action he is about to carry out. In this way the probability that the terrorist in a suicide mission will feel regret at the last minute is very low.

A study conducted on the quality (number of casualties per attack not the number of attacks) of Palestinian suicide terrorist attacks revealed findings that strengthen the complex link between suicide attacks and a range of factors in the suicide terrorist environment. It has been found that a high quality of terrorist attack may be linked to poverty, since when poverty spreads in society, terrorist activity is attractive to everyone, even to educated and skilled people. If so, high unemployment rates allow terrorist organizations to recruit educated, talented and experienced people relative to the general population. Such people can make a properly complex task and attack quality targets. Indeed, researchers who analyzed the population of suicide bombers in the Israeli-Palestinian conflict in the years 2000-2006 found a connection between economic conditions and the personal characteristics of the suicide terrorists and between quality targets of terrorist attacks.[201]

The power of associations

Nabil, a Fatah member who sends suicide bombers, came to the family in mourning for the person Nabil had sent to commit a suicide attack a few hours earlier. Nabil did not waste any time and started recruiting the next suicide bomber. Nabil told Anat Berko: "One exploded and one was caught at the central station...I brought to the house [of the parents of the suicide bomber] the tape of the suicide terrorist and I put in the video so they could watch...Darin Abu Aisha approached me several times. I sent her cousin to commit suicide and at her cousin's funeral she met me there." According to Nabil, despite his refusal, Darin begged him to carry out a suicide attack; for her to complete the mission successfully, she needed someone to supply the explosive belt and lead her to the scene. Talking a long time with Anat Berko, Nabil described the winding relationship with Darin, and the journey that eventually led Darin to blow herself up at a checkpoint near the city of Modi'in.[202]

Successful suicide attacks require the motivation of both the individual and the terrorist organization. A terrorist organization without activists willing to sacrifice themselves on the stand of the target will not be able to carry out suicide attacks. Herewith, even individuals with the motivation to carry out suicide attacks would find it difficult to do it well, because they will need the resources, knowledge and organizational ability necessary for performing a successful suicide attack.[203] Such an attack requires early planning, arms, selecting targets and implementation, and for all this the involvement of the terrorist organization is critical. Evidently, usually the terrorist suicide attacks were organized by terrorist organizations such as Hezbollah, the Tamil Tigers, Hamas, Islamic Jihad, and the PKK. Another reason for the importance of terrorist organization involvement is cultural - the cultures of the Middle East, Africa and Asia are less individual than Western cultures, and therefore the environmental and organizational impact on the suicide attack is greater. Execution and initiative of individuals outside the group and organizational context are less common. Therefore, the likelihood of personal despair or personal disorder of the individual being a key factor in suicide attacks is relatively low.[204]

For terrorist organizations that carry out suicide attacks to thrive and survive against a large military force, they must receive strong support from their community.[205] This is true for the execution of all attacks and terrorism of various kinds, not only to carry out suicide attacks. Terrorist organizations are locating and recruiting new volunteers who will be willing to sacrifice their lives for the cause of the group. Once volunteers are selected to carry out the suicide mission, terrorist organizations use a variety of means to keep them committed to performing the task. They share religious worship with them and record their statements before leaving to carry out an attack, so they remain committed to the mission, keep them isolated and carefully choose the people who will socialize with them before setting out on a mission.

There is also a cynical use of the cultural codes of Arab-Muslim society, which concern the dignity of women and their status in society. Many times, with the involvement of women in a suicide attack there is another woman in the background. That woman assists in recruiting the female suicide terrorist and accompanies them until the operation is carried out. This for example happened in Iraq, where a woman, usually older than the suicide bomber, was involved. She recruited them when they came to visit her daughters, and in some cases even made sure they would be raped. This made them think that the only way out of shame - the only way to honor them – was the execution of suicide attacks.[206]

Summary

The decision of terrorist organizations to launch a suicide attack campaign is the result of one or more factors: a sense that the political situation is at a standstill, a political crisis, competition among some terrorist organizations, previous suicide attacks, great social distance between the terrorist group to the attacked group and the culture of martyrdom. Two other factors were not discussed in the chapter: an asymmetrical conflict in which the weak side uses suicide attacks and violent and excessive government activity against terrorist organizations. When these conditions are met, the likelihood of a terrorist organization committing suicide attacks increases.[207]

It seems that the weight of the personal factors, including a personal crisis, has a relatively low weight compared to the other factors mentioned here. It seems that the organizations are the dominant factor in the growth of suicide terrorism.[208]

In addition, the findings regarding the connection between poverty, ignorance and committing a suicide attack are inconclusive and occupation alone is not a satisfactory condition to cause suicide terrorist attacks.

Tigers or Paper Tigers?

After the failure of the talks between Israel and the Palestinian Authority at Camp David in the summer of 2000, the Palestinian terrorist organizations began to strengthen and the terrorist attacks on Israel intensified - the security situation in Israel reached one of its worst levels. Attacks in those days of terror were up from the routine; among them - the murder of toddler Shalhevet Fass by a Palestinian sniper in Hebron; the murder of 21 young people in a suicide bombing at a dolphinarium club in Tel Aviv; the murder of 15 Israelis in a suicide bombing at the Sbarro restaurant in the center of Jerusalem - where most of the members of the Schijveschuurder family were murdered; the assassination of Minister Rehavam Ze'evi at a hotel in Jerusalem by a squad of the Popular Front for the Liberation of Palestine; the murder of 30 Israelis at the Park Hotel in Netanya on Passover Seder night; and the murder of Tali Hatuel and her four daughters by shooting at their car in Gush Katif. This partial list is only a fraction of the terrorist attacks of that period. From the outbreak of the second Intifada at the end of September 2000 to the end of 2004, the peak years of the Intifada,[209] 1,018 Israelis (about 46% of them in suicide attacks) were murdered and 5,760 were injured. For comparison, in the eleven years before (from

January 1, 1990 to September 28, 2000) about 344 people were killed in terrorist attacks in Israel.[210]

In the wake of the rising wave of terrorism, the heads of the council of the Israeli settlers in Judea, Samaria and Gaza ("Yesha Council") designed the slogan "Let the IDF win." They protested about the Oslo accords (the peace agreements between Israel and the Palestinians) and believed that the second Intifada was the event that marked the peace process's collapse. They sought to convey a message to the public and decision-makers that it was possible (and therefore also necessary) to eliminate Palestinian terrorism. In this message, they sought to put an end to the opposite common view, that the State of Israel was required to strive for a political settlement with the Palestinians and that withdrawal from the territories of Judea, Samaria and the Gaza Strip was the only way to stop the Palestinian terrorist attacks, as it was impossible to defeat terrorist organizations by force.

The opposite view can be found in retired brigadier general Aaron Bern: "If you do not hit the terrorists, who exploit every method of criminal action, we also will not fight a real war of attrition against terrorism, which is also accepted by the [political] left. [The Political] left can indeed claim it is impossible to defeat terrorism by force — a shallow claim, because there are more victories against terror than the opposite."[211]

In response to the slogan "Let the IDF win", two allegations were made. One was a denial that the IDF was restricted in its military activities. This is what retired Gen. Yom Tov Samia claimed: "It is nonsense to say such a thing. I am a commander of IDF forces in the Gaza Strip and the Southern Command, and I say to all the people of Israel: [...] I am taking all steps and actions that I think I need to take."[212] Another claim was that there are no magic solutions to deal with terrorism; therefore the solution will be achieved only through negotiations with the Palestinians and politically compromise achieved with the consent of both parties.[213]

The perception that it is impossible to defeat terrorist organizations is not only in the Israeli domain of public discourse. It often appears in statements by other non-Israeli sources. For example, a senior source at the European Commission was quoted: "The declaration of war on international terrorism - that design of Bush (the former president of the United States S.G) - is an empty and stupid statement. It is clear to all who deal with the issue that it is impossible to fight terrorism, it is impossible to declare a war on it and probably it is not possible to defeat terrorism by purely military means."[214] Therefore, this chapter will focus mainly on these questions: Are terrorist organization as successful as many tend to think? Or, to put it another way, is terrorism the "winning formula" for achieving political goals, such as successfully forcing the opponent to achieve its political objectives? Do terrorist organizations manage to survive for long time? And finally, are violent means (the army, the police and the intelligence agencies) effective in suppressing the terrorist organizations? This chapter will not deal with questions related to the achievement of short-term tactical goals or the effectiveness of various terrorist attacks, such as kidnappings versus the use of bombs (except for the discussion of suicide terrorism). The chapter will also not deal with the effectiveness of tactics used for the repression of terrorist organizations.

The triumphal arch

The triumphal arch originated in Roman architecture, where they were used to commemorate military victories, to glorify the rulers and to mark important events such as the coronation of a new emperor. In his book "Wars of the Jews", Josephus Flavius (Joseph Ben Matityahu) described the march of victory of Titus and the Roman emperor Vespasian, following the crushing of the Jewish revolt and the destruction of Jerusalem by Titus: "The like prayers did Titus put up also. After which prayers Vespasian made a short speech to all the people; and then sent away the soldiers to a dinner prepared for them by the emperor. Then did he retire to that gate, which was called the gate of the pomp, because pompous shows do always go through that gate. There it was that they tasted some food: and when they had put on their triumphal garments and had offered sacrifices to the gods that were placed at the gate, they sent the triumph forward, and marched through the theatres."[215]

Victory gates are usually decorated with inscriptions and various shapes. Nor is Titus' triumphal arch - built about twelve years after his conquest of Judea in 82 (ACE) – unusual.

On my visit to Rome, I went to visit the Titus Gate. The Titus Gate is in the center of ancient Rome (the Roman Forum), not far from the Roman Colosseum, where the battles of the gladiators took place. For me the visit to the Titus Gate was moving and of profound significance, a reminder of the national and religious destruction of the Jewish people after the Great Revolt. At this gate, on its inner side, is carved Titus' coronation ceremony; on the other side is a parade of the Jewish captives, bearing the temple vessels, and particularly evident is the temple lamp (The Menora).

This is what Yosef ben Matityahu wrote about the march of the Jewish captives: "[...] and then also select from the Jewish captives to Simon and John even seven hundred higher and better looking from the rest of their brethren, and commanded to carry them soon easy to Italy, that was with his heart to ornament in honor his chariot at his victory day [...] Even the Jewish captives came dressed in jewels and a variety of colored garments spectacular to the eyes so that all show ... the glory of the beauty of the sight of them ... And for the other spoils they were carried in great plenty. But for those that were taken in the temple of Jerusalem, they made the greatest figure of them all. That is the golden table, of the weight of many talents. The candlestick also, that was made of gold."[216]

Indeed, Titus's victory was a very clear one. He destroyed the political and religious center of the Jews, killing them in masse and some of the survivors he took into slavery. The results of the uprising were on the scale of a real Holocaust for the Jewish people; after him, the Roman rule in the Roman Province, which they gave the name Palestina to, was stronger than ever. Herewith, not all wars and rebellions ended in clear cut victories as in the case of the Romans' victory over the Jews in their homeland.

The issue of defining victory or success in war is complex, varies from period to period and depends on the subjective perceptions of the warring parties. Many times, success in war is measured by the degree of success of one side overpowering the other side and defeating it. Herewith, success in war is measured not only by military concepts, but according to the diplomatic results of the war and achieving a better political reality than the one that was before the war.

At the military level one's achievement is the other's loss, whereas in political outcomes the relationship is more complex. When seeking control over a particular area, it is easy to see the results of the war. However, achievements may also be reflected in non-territorial arrangements, and in such cases, it is more difficult to determine who won the war.

Moreover, it is possible to succeed in a war without a military victory, and this happens when the desired political achievement is achieved without defeating the enemy. When the goal is survival or defense, thwarting enemy efforts without improving the pre-war situation may also be considered a success. Moreover, sometimes military achievements are not translated into political achievements, for example in cases where the defeated party does not receive dictates regarding its vital interests, although he is inferior on the battlefield.

The achievements in war can be divided into short-term tactical achievements and intermediate achievements. Interim achievements should help achieve the strategic goals, which are the stated and long-term goals of the leadership. If so, the success or victory of terrorist organizations is measured by the degree to which the strategic goal stated by the leaders of the organizations has been achieved, which was the reason for the establishment of the organization and the motivation for its struggle.

Terrorism is a strategy of attrition, and tactical achievements are supposed to help the organization achieving its long-term political goals. Tactical achievements of terrorist organizations may include mobilizing the support of the local population, eroding the internal resilience of the targeted country, media coverage, partial political concessions, disrupting the political process, raising money, mobilizing activists and gaining international legitimacy. Strategic political goals of terrorist organizations are national, ethnic, separatist, religious (Islamic, Christian and other), revolutionary, fascist, anarchist or targets on any subject, such as opposition to animal experiments.

This chapter will discuss the degree of strategic success of terrorist organizations. According to the rational model terrorist organizations act strategically in calculated ways to achieve their political objectives and tactical goals.[217] The degree of effectiveness of terrorism as a strategy is measured by the degree of success in achieving the strategic goals declared by the terrorist organization, such as the establishment of a Kurdish state, the expulsion foreign forces from Iraq, the establishment of an Islamic caliphate in the East Mediterranean area. etc.

Another reason is that in asymmetric conflicts, such as a conflict between a state and a non-state organization, the terrorist organization may achieve its political goals even if it suffers heavy losses. Each organization is required to maintain even limited military capability and harass the country being fought through terrorist attacks.[218] If so, the degree of success of a terrorist organization is examined by its ability to achieve its long-term political goals. The victory of the state come through stopping the activities of the terrorist organization without allowing it to achieve its long-term, strategic and political goals. The way states do it is by suppression of the military wing of the organization, going after its assets and killing, imprisoning or exiling its leaders.

Terrorism is inherently a violent strategy. It is an attempt to impose on the opponent a policy appropriate to the preferences of the terrorist organization, as they appeared in the organization's manifesto and in the statements of its leaders. If so, the degree of success of terrorist organizations is measured by the degree of their success in fulfilling their policy requirements. Terrorist organizations may achieve all their goals, achieve them only partially or achieve minor achievements, equivalent to failure. Examples of the failure of the terrorist organization are its dissolution, liquidation or cessation of activity without political achievements.

It should also be noted that the success of terrorist organizations is not only measured by the extent to which all (or most) of their strategic objectives are achieved, but also by the extent of the strategic impact on important political events. A few examples of successes of this type: the September 11 attacks have affected the foreign policy of the United States, the terrorist attacks in Madrid influenced the results of the election and ended Spain's support of the war in Iraq (however the strategic influence of this attack is disputed),[219] the terrorist campaign of the Palestinians in the early 2000s led to the collapse of the Oslo accords and more. However, as defined above, this chapter is not focused on these types of achievements of terrorist organizations.

Moreover, wars are usually waged according to one of two strategies: determination or attrition. Determination strives to destroy the enemy and subdue him in as short a time as possible. Attrition is designed to erode the enemy's power, causing him moral and material fatigue, until he is worn out and becomes exhausted gradually and slowly. Attrition strategies are usually adopted when there is not the power required to reach a determination; sometimes it is done with no choice, sometimes it is a deliberate strategy.

Terrorism is a distinct attrition strategy. The attacks are limited in scope relative to fighting large scale conventional wars and aimed mainly toward civilians. The purpose of the terrorist organization is to intimidate the enemy state and exhaust the country which is fighting him. The bloodshed and with it the fear of the citizens is a way to gradually erode the resilience of the citizens and decision-makers.

One of the most notable differences between attrition and determination is the time dimension. In the determination the ambition is to reach a battle that will collapse the enemy, if possible, by one move, a battle that will lead to the end of the war. In attrition the violence causes the enemy a cumulative damage. Admittedly the determinate war may also be lengthy, but the ambition is to end the war as quickly as possible. In contrast, attrition is deliberately slow, and those adopting this strategy must be patient and demonstrate resilience over time.

Moreover, the goals of terrorist organizations, that some researchers consider as the measure for success, may be organizational achievements, such as maintaining and expanding the base of support, increasing the resources available to the organization, maintaining organizational unity and preventing defection to opponent organizations. Certainly, the most basic organizational task of any terrorist organization is to survive for years and not end its life in an internal split. For the attrition strategy to succeed, terrorist organizations are supposed to survive for many years. Hence the time dimension is critical to the success of terrorist organizations. "Successful" terrorist organizations are therefore supposed to wage lengthy struggles and survive against the oppression of the states which are fighting them, save themselves from internal dissolution and make successful terrorist attacks over many years.[220]

The birth of the "invincible terrorist"

After World War II, the days of the French and British empires came to an end. The empires of the past were replaced by two superpowers, the United States of America and the Soviet Union. During this period, global changes began in the international system. One of them was the process of decolonization, a process in which the European powers, France and Britain, withdraw their domination almost entirely from all the colonies which were under their control in Africa, the Middle East and the Far East. Then the legend about the "invincible terrorist" was born.

Anti-colonial struggles for national liberation, a series of terrorist campaigns mainly against British and French rule in most of the colonies, included the struggle to end the British mandate on the land of Israel/Palestine, the struggle to end the British control in Cyprus, the struggle against French domination in Algeria and the fight against British control over Aden and the Suez Canal, etc. The series of successes of the anti-colonial campaigns by guerrilla movements or terrorist organizations for about a decade and a half generated the myth about the invincible terrorist. However, the four anti-colonial campaigns mentioned above were exceptional and did not testify to the rule, as in these cases there were unique characteristics that helped the rebels.

These were the years after World War II. The long war exhausted the resources of the powers; it took the lives of millions of civilians and soldiers from European countries. The public and governments of the colonial powers therefore had no ambition to conquer these countries, sacrifice human lives and waste resources. As well, the anti-colonial movements had broad public support among the local population in the colonies, support that is not necessarily common among terrorist organizations.[221]

For evidence, if we divide 20th century terrorism into four waves of (Anarchist, National and Anti-colonial, Marxist and Religious) we will see that only the anti-colonial wave had an impressive success for terrorist organizations. In the rest the situation was a complete failure or at most a limited success.[222] It is worth remembering that in the 20th century the British were able to defeat several rebellions in their colonies (although most of them never experienced a significant terrorist campaign),[223] such as the Arab uprising, the Boer War in South Africa, the rebellion of the Mau-Mau in Kenya and communist uprising in Malaysia, so actually, despite the conventional wisdom, the balance of success and failure of colonial powers in repressing rebellions was not necessarily prone to failure.

However, generally the colonial powers did not remain in control of the colonies overseas, but the reasons were broader than the threat of terrorism per se. After War World II governments and public in the motherlands of the colonial powers disliked war in general and colonial wars. The public in these countries never had any desire to sacrifice the lives of their soldiers to go on and dominate overseas areas. Colonialism and imperialism were no longer legitimate goals, and there was no vital national interest at stake. Imperial ambitions were replaced by feelings of guilt all relating to the exploitation, oppression and domination of the European countries in all sorts of places around the world. This discouraged the Europeans from continuing military control on their colonies.[224]

If so, the invincible terrorist myth may be fed on the one hand by facts, which are true in themselves, but do not give an overall and accurate picture, and on the other hand from some notable cases, which are not necessarily representative, but they are mentioned again and again and thus the myth continues. Later we will discuss how the image of the success of terrorist organizations has a foothold and consider the view of scholars of terrorism regarding the claim that terrorism is a successful strategy.

As the lifespan of a butterfly?

Many times, the argument that butterflies live only one day is heard, but it turns out that this is only a myth. The "Little Blue" (Tiny Azure) butterfly passes all three incarnations - egg, larva, and pupa - lays its eggs a day after release from its cocoon and dies before the age of three days. However, the Tiny Azure does not represent the common lifespan of butterflies.

At the other end of the scale is the "Great Wanderer Monarch", which can reach seven to eight months.[225] Herewith, both the famous Great Monarch butterfly and the Little Blue one, which lives only few days, do not represent the common longevity in the world of butterflies. The common lifespan of a butterfly in the wild after reaching the adult stage is two to four weeks.[226]

Many times, when people think about terrorist organizations, they think immediately about the most famous terrorist organizations, the largest ones the "Great Monarchs" of terrorism world, and therefore people believe that terrorist organizations survive for a long time. As of 2022, the terrorist organizations that come to our minds easily - due to being the most famous, active for many years - are organizations like Hezbollah (39 years), Al-Qaeda (34), etc. But these organizations do not represent the entire population of terrorist organizations. According to Rapoport, about 90% of modern terrorist organizations survive less than a year. About half of those who survive more than a year no longer exist in the year of their 10th anniversary.

The struggle of successful terrorist organizations usually lasts for several generations, most prominent of which are the Palestine Liberation Organization (PLO) and the Irish Republican Army (IRA). Indeed, the percentage of terrorist organizations that survive more than forty years is about 4%,[227] this means that about

96% of the terrorist organizations live less than 40 years. A similar finding was found when checking the life of terrorist organizations in the years 1970 to 2007. It was found that terrorist organizations which survived for more than 30 years have been in the top decile of the terrorist world. That is, they survived longer than 90% of terrorist organizations. Additionally, throughout the life average of all terrorist organizations is about one-third the length of the life of these organizations (12 vs. 36).[228]

In a follow-up study, Khusrav Gaibulloev and Todd Sandler analyzed a higher number of terrorist organizations (586) and found that while Rapoport's evaluation about 90% "death" in the first year was excessive, it definitely had a similar distribution. Gaibulloev and Sandler found that about 25% of terrorist organizations in their sample did not survive their first year; a little more than 66% survived 10 years at most. The average age of terrorist organizations was about 10 years, and about half of those who survived the first year did not survive till their 10th year.[229]

It should be noted that the distribution of terrorist organizations' lifetime is not random. Moreover, it is possible to formulate a mathematical expression that reflects exponential distribution. According to that mathematical expression there is a relation, defined in the formula, between the length of life and the probability of a terrorist organization to reach a certain age.[230]

For example, the Underground Weather organization survived for about nine years. Their special name is derived from the title of their first publication in 1969 - "You don't need a weatherman to know which way the wind blows", a line taken from Bob Dylan's song, Subterranean Homesick Blues. This terrorist organization was a group of American citizens, with extreme leftist worldviews, who opposed American imperialism, whose system oppressed peoples and groups around the world. The organization operated in the United States until 1977, during this time it attacked government institutions, Congress members, academic institutions, banks and more. Apparently, during their relatively short period of activity, the average number of activists was no more than 15. The organization still managed to split into the "Central Committee" and the "Revolutionary Committee" and ceased to operate due to activity of the American police and the FBI.[231]

The average of terrorist organizations' lifetime is misleading because a few terrorist organizations that have survived for decades are leaning the overall average upward. Hence the figure worth focusing on is the median (the number that half of the data is below it and half is above it) and not the average.

To understand the importance of the median and the upward bias of the average, I will give an example of average income. First, we will explain what the median salary is: this is a representative amount that half of the employees earn more from it - and the other half, earn less from it. Therefore, the median salary is considered by many economists a representative number, better than the average, in reflecting the economic state of the public. For example, we say that the median salary is 1500 US$ a month only, yet at the same time the average salary is at about 2500 US$. This happened because there are many people that earn very low salary but few people that earn very high salary. The people who earn a very high salary draw the average salary upwards and skew the distribution of incomes. Therefore, the median not the average is more accurate in this case to understand the real economic situation.

Like the average income, the average longevity of terrorist organizations is skewed upwards. As we have seen, the terrorist organizations that have survived for decades are few, but because they survive far more than most terrorist organizations the average life expectancy of all terrorist organizations is much higher. Hence the average is not a more reliable figure for understanding the situation than the median lifespan (number that half of the terrorist organizations live below it and half above it).

The graph below illustrates the distribution of life expectancy of terrorist organizations. The continuous line represents the distribution of the total number of terrorist organizations that ceased to operate in the years 1968-2006 and the dashed line represents the number of terrorist organizations that ceased to exist after a filtering of organizations that ended their life by internal splits. The reason for this division is due to the fact that sometimes parts of splintered terrorist organizations continued to carry out terrorist activities under a different name. The inclusion of terrorist organizations that have ceased to exist due to splitting may therefore create a misleading picture. The graph shows that the distribution in both cases is almost identical, the largest group of organizations (about 40% of all organizations and 30% without organizations that have split). The graph has a long "tail", representing a very limited number of organizations, which operated for many years. According to the data shown in the graph, the average lifespan of terrorist organizations was about seven years and when organizations that have split were filtered, the average life expectancy increased to nine years. However, as mentioned above, the more important figure is the median: only three years of life for all terrorist organizations; four and half years when filtering the terrorist organizations that have split. In another words, 50% of terrorist organizations survived three years or less!232 When examining the group of organizations that survived up to 10 years, it was find that most terrorist organizations, about 66% of them, survived for six years or less.

Figure 4: Distribution of the Terrorist Organizations Lifespan 1968-2006[233]

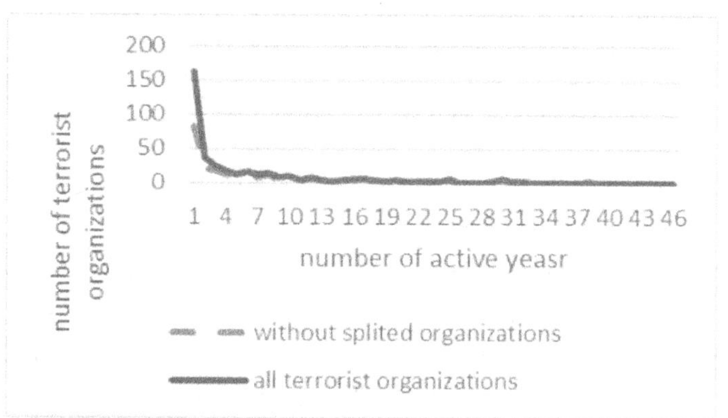

The data presented here reappeared in all the studies that examined the survival of terrorist organizations, even when tested hundreds of terrorist organizations and when tested two thousand, even when tested at all terrorist organizations and when analyzing only those who carried out trans-national attacks. The distribution was maintained even when used in databases that differ from each other and when examined with several forms of measuring the survival of terrorist organizations.

From all these studies it seems that the largest group of terrorist organizations survived one year or less. That group is 26%-68% of terrorist organizations, and the median lifetime is one to three years only (depends on the study).[234]

Back to the world of butterflies. A large part of the terrorist organizations are the "little blue butterflies", while the "big monarchs" of the terrorist organizations which live for many years, are the exception among terrorist organizations. Yet, they are the ones that attract the attention and give a misleading feeling that all terrorist organizations are like them.

Terrorist organizations rely on attrition, and it usually takes a long time for them to be effective. We can see that the terrorist organizations which won their struggle survived longer than the terrorist organizations that did not achieve their goals. Indeed, the median lifespan of terrorist organizations which won is considerably higher than the median lifespan of the terrorist organizations that were defeated (8 vs. 4), and the differences between these two groups of terrorist organizations is even statistically significant.[235] Also according to a study by Audrey Cronin the percentage of successful terrorist organizations was relatively higher among terrorist organizations which survived 40 years or more.[236]

Furthermore, not only do most terrorist organizations fail to survive beyond a few years, 20% of them end their lives because of organizational splitting. Although these findings are not sufficient to validate the claim that long-term survival increases the likelihood of victory, these findings indicate the importance of the time dimension in the attrition strategy, hence the importance of lifetime and the importance of the relatively short life of most terrorist organizations.

In conclusion, a small minority of terrorist organizations survive for a long time, just as the Great Wandering Monarch lifetime does not represent most butterfly's lifespans. In fact, the myth about the longevity of terrorist organizations is the opposite of the myth about the longevity of the butterfly: according to the myth, the butterfly lives a shorter life, but actually it lives longer. On the contrary, terrorist organizations seem to survive for decades, but in fact only a small number of them live for such a long time.

A short-lived life does not necessarily indicate that terrorist organizations do not win or that terrorism is not a success story in the political sense. Some from the short-lived terrorist organizations succeeded in achieving their goals, and others, who survived for a long time, failed in doing so. The relatively short lives of most terrorist organizations still do not prove that the terrorist organizations are not a success story. We will discuss this in the next part of the chapter.

Is terrorism a success story?

In 1956 spoke Mao Zedong, the former leader of China and the Chinese Communist Party, met with two well-known people from Latin America and said to them: "Now the imperialism of the United States [seems] strong but, it is not. Politically it is very weak because it is separate from the masses and is not cherished by anybody, not even by the people in the United States. They seem to be powerful but, they are not something to be afraid of, they are paper tigers ... A tiger, made of paper, is unable to withstand wind and rain. I believe that the United States is nothing more than a paper tiger."[237]

Of course, Mao's remarks were exaggerated and involved anti-American communist propaganda. He meant, however, that the United States should not be feared, since it is not as threatening as it seems at a first glance. Mao used the image of a "paper tiger", an image that indicates something that seems threatening, but is harmless and need not be feared. Are terrorist organizations really paper tigers? Perhaps they are real tigers, threatening their enemies, and thus succeed in achieving their goals? In other words, is terrorism a successful strategy?

We should note that some researchers analyzed individual test cases and did not reach clear conclusions; Yet most studies examining many cases have consistently found that a very small proportion of terrorist organizations have succeeded in achieving their goals. Regarding the 1980s and early 1990s, a group of scholars claimed that few terrorist organizations managed to achieve their long-term goals, therefore it can be concluded that terrorism is a failed strategy.[238] However, they did not conduct a thorough empirical examination. In addition, there are studies that discussed the government's response and the degree of its success in suppressing terrorism, but most of them were studies that built theoretical and mathematical models and did not conduct a data analysis.[239]

Several studies have examined individual instances or examples given from the 20th century history and found that most of the terrorist organizations, which ended their activity, did not achieve their goals,[240] including the "Ulster Volunteer Force",[241] "The Naxalite", which the government of India eradicated, and the Irish Republican Army (IRA), which stopped terrorism after a political process without expelling the British from Northern Ireland.[242]

In her doctoral dissertation Limor Noble analyzed eight cases and concluded that terrorist organizations only partially managed to achieve their strategic goals, among other things, because they became a political entity, like, for example, Fatah, the IRA (Irish Republican Army), Hezbollah and the Muslim Brotherhood in Egypt. The rest of the organizations which surveyed did not achieve strategic objectives at all.[243]

However, studies that examined one case study or a very small number of cases, as well as in studies that used only demonstrations, found that terrorism was effective in achieving political goals.[244] For example, Alan Dershowitz whose analysis focused on just one case, the Palestinian Liberation Organization (PLO), claimed that the organization was a success due to political achievements caused by terrorist attacks.[245] However, it is worth remembering that the achievements of the PLO were only tactical but not the fulfillment of strategic political goals such as gaining international political legitimacy (although it was one of the deadliest and most global terrorist organizations in the 20th century).[246] In the same breath Dershowitz mentioned several other organizations who failed at all their aims or succeeded to a lesser extent only, such as the Kurdish Workers Party (PKK) and the Irish Republican Army (IRA).

Another study, about the Palestinian terrorism in 1988-2006, found that Palestinian terrorism forced Israel to make territorial concessions to the Palestinians.[247] The Israeli-Palestinian conflict has continued though, and therefore it is impossible to say clearly whether the PLO achieved its strategic objectives. It can only determine that the PLO managed to survive and achieved its long-term objectives partially.

In the studies cited so far, there is not a single study that has systematically examined the overall picture of the terrorism world. In all studies cited, the researchers examined only one case or a small number of cases; sometimes they relied on examples and theoretical research. Yet, examination of one case or a small number of cases does not allow us to see the situation overall and conclude about broad trends. Moreover, the case selection, especially in studies examining a small number of cases, may skew the results of the study. In addition, in studies that examined a small number of cases, researchers re-examined the same organizations again and again, including Hamas, Hezbollah, Fatah, the Tamil Tigers and the IRA.

Only in the last decade have terrorism investigators begun to examine the overall picture of the terrorist world in terms of the success of terrorist organizations. For example, Max Abrams expanded the number of cases and examined 125 violent campaigns conducted by violent non-governmental organizations (not just those which deliberately killed civilians like terrorist organizations) and concluded that terrorist organizations (organizations that deliberately kill civilians as a strategy) are less successful than guerrilla movements (which manly fought the security forces) when it comes to subduing governments. Although in 30% of cases the organization succeeded in subduing the government (usually in partial success), but in this study only one case, of over a hundred cases, the organization was a terrorist organization.[248]

Similar findings emerged when examining civil wars in which the rebel organization used a terrorist strategy.[249] According to another study, there was not one case of rebellious organization which won the civil war through terrorism. In contrast 22% of the cases that did not use terrorism, ended in victory for the rebellious organization.[250] This conclusion that terrorism is not a successful strategy, was found in all the studies in which hundreds of cases were analyzed.[251]

The clear conclusion that emerges from the concise review is that the success of terrorist organizations is rare and stands at a maximum of 10% of all cases. If so, why do people continue to form terrorist organizations and try to achieve political goals through terrorism? Some believe that terrorist organizations are irrational, so they are turning to terrorism even though it is not an effective strategy. However, there may be other reasons. In the 20th century, there have been several notable cases of successful terrorist campaigns, as well as a few successful guerrilla wars that have created an aura of guerrilla success, such as in China, Vietnam, Cuba, Afghanistan and Somalia. These cases have created heroic figures such as Ernesto Che Guevara, figures who have inflamed the imagination of the masses around the world. Some of them even decided to imitate the activities of these organizations. Sometimes the leaders of terrorist organizations get confused between the terrorist tactics and guerrilla warfare. Whereas the tactics of guerrilla warfare - aimed primarily at security forces - are quite successful, they establish terrorist organizations, though the efficiency of terrorism in achieving political goals is very limited.[252]

Sometimes terrorist organizations strive to achieve tactical goals and succeed in doing so. Thus, people who turn to terrorist activity cultivate the hope that if they persevere in their struggle and accumulate tactical successes, they will eventually succeed in achieving their strategic goal. Moreover, the political motivation of terrorists is very high, and therefore even if reasonable success is low, terrorists will try to achieve their goals.

The next section is focused on the use of an extraordinary means - suicide terrorism - and discusses the claim that terrorist organizations believe that this is a successful tactic.

Suicide all the way to success?

As we have seen so far, terrorism is usually not a successful strategy and most terrorist organizations do not survive more than a few years, and many do not survive even more than one year. However, one question remains open: Is suicide terrorism effective in achieving political strategic goals?

As mentioned, suicide terrorism has clear tactical advantages over conventional terrorism: it is simple, does not require an escape route, guarantees a large rate of casualties and extensive damage. It is possible to know in advance what the exact location will be or the time the bomb will explode. Also, the psychological impact of suicide terrorism is greater than a normal terrorist act due to feelings of helplessness among the public and decision makers.[253]

Ehud Sprinzak and Robert Pape studied effectiveness of suicide terrorism.[254] In his book Dying to Win Pape study comprehensively cases examined recently in Sprintzak's work, therefore, I discuss here only Pape's study.[255] Pape examined 18 Suicide terrorist campaigns around the world that happened in the years 1980-2003, including thirteen campaigns that have finished already. Pape found that in seven cases the terrorist organizations succeeded in achieving their goals, and he believed that these successes encouraged terrorist organizations to continue using suicide bombers. The terrorist organizations were the expulsion of American and French forces from Lebanon in 1983, the withdrawal of Israel to the security zone in 1985, the withdrawal of IDF forces from most of the Gaza Strip and cities in Judea and Samaria in 1995-1994, the release of Hamas leader Sheikh Yassin in 1997, the Sri Lankan government agreeing to establish a Tamil independent state in 1990, declaration of Kurdish autonomy in the Late 1990s and Change of Status of the Tamil Region in Sri Lanka in 2001.

According to Pape, in almost all cases success came after the suicide attacks began and not before. The leaders of the terrorist organizations, sometimes also the leaders of the countries, linked the success of terrorist organizations to suicide attacks.

Pape also examined the 13 cases already ended and found six cases there was no achievement to terrorist organizations attempts to Hezbollah to the Israeli army withdrawal from the security zone in south Lebanon in the years 1985-1986, Hamas's terrorist attacks in 1996 in response to the assassinations carried out by Israel, the Indian control of Punjab, terrorist activity of Tamil tigers in Sri Lanka in 1995 to 2002 and the two suicide terror campaigns of the Kurdish Workers Party (PKK) between 1996 and 1999. The cases of failure are almost identical to cases of success, but Pape noted that about 50% of the successes were much more from the overall success rate of terrorist attacks. If so, could suicide terrorism, unlike terrorism in general, succeed in achieving terrorist organizations' strategic goals?

An in-depth look at the findings of the study shows that the picture is more complex than Pape presents, since the success cases do not mean successes in achieving the strategic political goals of the terrorist organizations but only tactical and partial successes. Pape noted that "most of the terrorists' successes were modest, did not involve key interests of security or economic prosperity of the target state and most could be annulled [by the target state].[256] In other words, suicide terrorism, by itself, cannot lead to victory in the strategic sense we are discussing in this chapter.

For example, the United States' presence in Lebanon has been largely humanitarian and has not been linked to vital American interests. Israel withdrew from Lebanon in the mid-1980s but remained for a decade and a half in the security zone in southern Lebanon (although the most suicide attacks perpetrated by Hezbollah occurred in the mid-1980s). Furthermore, while Israel withdrew from territory it controlled, and gave it to the Palestinians, it did so after signing the Oslo Accords with the PLO. Israel believed that in the spirit of the agreements with the PLO, the Palestinian Authority would control these areas and prevent future terrorist attacks. On this Pape wrote: "Suicide attacks to achieve more ambitious goals were doomed to failure and provoked aggressive military responses".[257] A striking example of the conclusion of Pape is operation

Defensive Shield. The operation began on Passover 2002. After Passover evening the terrorist committed a suicide massacre killing tens of Jews in their Passover holiday feast (the Seder), at the Park Hotel in Netanya. Israel's drastic retaliation came after a year and a half of a massive terrorist campaign by the Palestinians, in which the Palestinians carried out dozens of suicide attacks on the citizens of Israel and its soldiers.

If we focus on a few details regarding the success of suicide terrorism, it seems that even the claim to tactical or partial successes does not stand on solid ground. Terrorist organizations carry out attacks while perpetrating regular terrorist attacks, and it is very difficult to discern the impact of suicide attacks alone.

Also, the number of cases presented in Pape's study is largely artificial, as successful suicide attacks are only an intermediate target for terrorist organizations. Terrorist organizations strive to achieve long-term political goals, and this study has not examined any such goals. Additionally, the separation into several suicide campaigns increases the absolute number of successes. If we look at the number of terrorist organizations that have acted and separate the cases only according to the countries they fought against, we will find that in total Pape analyzed only five cases: Hezbollah against the multinational force in Lebanon, Hezbollah against Israel, Hamas against Israel, the Tamil Tigers against Sri Lanka, the Babbar Khalsa International (BKI) against India and the Kurdish Workers' Party (PKK) against Turkey. Focusing only on these five cases there was full success only in one case: eviction the multi-national forces from Lebanon. this case is the exception. This is the only case where the powers sent their forces across the ocean for humanitarian mission participated in a

non-domestic war that took place not on their
doorstep. It should be noted that in the case of the
Tamil Tigers, the Sri Lankan army eventually managed
to suppress them.[258] Moreover, Abrams, whose study
quoted above, examined also the reasons for the
success of terrorist organizations and he did not found
a significant correlation between the use of suicide
bombers and the success of terrorist organizations.[259]
Therefore, suicide terrorism is a strategy that hardly
succeeds in achieving the political goals of terrorist
organizations. At most, in some cases, it may lead to
tactical and partial achievements.[260]

Can terrorist organizations be defeated?[261]

"After a Quarter of a Century: The Tamil Tigers
Surrendered." This was the headline on one of the news
websites on May 17, 2009.[262] For the first time since
1983, Sri Lanka's military ruled the entire island. The
leader of the Tigers of Tamil Eelam, Velupillai
Prabhakaran, was killed while trying to escape in an
ambulance under the dark of the night. Before him the
military killed his heir-son Anthony, the commander of
the Tamil Tigers' air force. "This battle has reached its
bitter end... We have decided to silence our guns. Our
only regrets are for the lives lost and that we could not
hold out for longer." This was a message posted on the
website of the Tamil Tigers or the full name Liberation
Tigers of Tamil Eelam (LTTE).[263]

A terrorist organization that fought for the separation from
Sri Lanka and the establishment of a Tamil state for 26
years. The Sri Lankan government rejected the Tamil

rebels' declaration of a unilateral ceasefire and said there was no justification for stopping the fighting against the rebels, certainly a step away from the destruction of the LTTE in its territory.

The Sri Lankan army eliminated one of the most powerful terrorist organizations that operated in the 20th and the beginning of the 21st century. The prolonged conflict started in the beginning of the 1970s but turned to a massive terrorist campaign on the 1980s in which have been killed in Sri Lanka at least 100,000 peoples, including 40,000 people in the last months of fighting.[264]

Most of the Sri Lankan population is Sinhalese and believes in Buddhism. Tamils believe in Hinduism and make up about 12% of the population; the rest are Muslims. The Sinhalese majority sought to impose its language and religion on all of Sri Lanka while discriminating against the Tamils in all aspects of life. In 1972, when Sri Lanka became independent, it established a constitution. Buddhism was the main religion, and the academic and political activity of the Tamils were limited. Possibly this was the signal for the growth of the Tamil uprising.

In 1976 Velupillai Prabhakaran founded the Liberation Tigers of Tamil Eelam and was the leader of the organization until its eradication. At the beginning, the organization called for the recognition of the Hindu religion and the Tamil language and appropriate Tamil representation in the public sphere of Sri Lanka. Later, LTTE adopted a separatist ideology and demanded the establishment of an independent Tamil state in northern Sri Lanka and the northeast of the country.

The organization established its position among the Tamils and at its peak the organization's military strength was estimated at about 18,000 fighters, including about 1,600 children (there were even estimates that about 60% of fighters of the organization was under the age of 18). The organization conducted a terrorist campaign of politicians and civilians' assassinations. Until the American invasion to Iraq in 2003, the Tamil Tigers were the terrorist organization that carried out the highest number of suicide attacks.

Members of the organization murdered the Prime Minister of Sri Lanka, the Prime Minister of India, and in attack that aimed at killing of the President of Sri Lanka 20 civilians were killed and they almost managed to kill the president (in this attack the President of Sri Lanka lost his eye). The organization also attacked the convoy of the Chief of Staff of the Sri Lankan Army.

The organization had a naval arm with mini-submarines and an air force with light aircrafts. The organization also had a women's brigade, and a suicide unit of men and women and a cyber warfare unit. The sources of funding for the Tamil Tigers were donations from the Tamil diaspora around the world alongside extensive criminal activity of hard drugs trade. According to estimations, the organization had efficient branches of fundraising and propaganda in more than 50 countries and raised each year 200-300 million dollars. The Tamil Tigers had extensive ties with other terrorist organizations, such as the PLO, Hezbollah, Hamas and the Popular Front for the Liberation of Palestine.

In 2000, there was already a de facto state in the northern provinces of Sri Lanka - Tamil Eelam. In 2001, the Tigers announced on a unilateral ceasefire and even signed a joint memorandum of understanding with the government of Sri Lanka. However, the organization continued to act violently, fulfilled unsuccessful rounds of negotiations between the governments of Sri Lanka the Tamil Tigers and caused serious damage to the economy of the country. These were some of the reasons why Sri Lankan President Mahinda Rajapaksa declared a comprehensive war on the organization. Although the war severely affected tens of thousands of civilians, it led to the elimination of a terrorist organization that operated with great success for several decades.

This case shows that even a terrorist organization with very impressive capabilities and which were active for a long time, may be defeated by violent means. The obvious question is whether the case of the Tamil Tigers is an exceptional case that does not attest to the rule? The question is whether other countries are capable of coping with terrorist organizations and eradicating them by military means? The debate over the question whether indeed it is possible to defeat terrorist organizations relies on world views about the desired extent use of violent means: It is customary to distinguish between Hawkish tougher positions and Dovish or more compromising positions. Therefore, the question about the ability to cop militarily with terrorist organizations is a question that concerns political positions in the first place, so for the most part the public discussion does not revolve around data. At most, each side brings selective examples, which strengthen his position. In this section, which seals the chapter and the entire book, the data provide a broad picture on the success rate in suppressing terrorist organizations found by scientific studies on many terrorist organizations.

Several theoretical studies have discussed various strategies for coping with terrorism.[265] Another research group discussed the question of the ability to deter terrorist organizations, using a strategy of delivering costs to terrorist organizations or threat of punishment. The answer to this question is controversial but has been examined using individual test cases or examples only.[266] Other studies have shown violent repressive measures of the military, or the police were effective, but also examined individual cases or just mentioned examples.[267] Among the scholars there is no consensus on the effective means of repressing terrorist organizations.

For example, two studies were conducted on the way Israel coped with terrorism after the outbreak of the second Intifada (uprising) in September 2000: One of Yoaz Handel and Zaki Shalom - "Let the IDF Win – The Slogan that fulfilled Itself" - and one study of Nadav Morag. Their conclusion was the same: Israel managed to defeat the second Intifada. Morag used seven criteria: reduction The number of civilians affected, economic struggle, social resilience, the international and internal status of the government and the weakening of support for the Palestinian leadership. Based on these seven criteria, Morag concluded that Israel had successfully cope with the Palestinian terrorism in the second Intifada.[268]

Another study analyzed the Israeli policy in the years 1987-2004, but the conclusions were different. The study examined the extent of the effect of punitive and conciliatory actions against Palestinian terrorist activity.

No effect was found for repressive actions. On the contrary, they were counterproductive and have been related to an increase in the number of terrorist attacks. However, Israel's reconciliating actions were associated with a reduction in terrorist activity.[269]

Case studies have their methodological advantages, but the answer to the question of whether terrorism can be suppressed by violent means lies in the large numbers. Is the proportion of terrorist organizations that ended their activities after the state used violent means against them - considerably smaller? Are the cases in which the state defeats terrorist organizations so rare so it can be said that terrorism cannot be defeated?

The discussion hereinafter is mainly based on the research of Seth Jones and Martin Libicki. They studied the ways in which terrorist organizations ended their activity. They examined 648 terrorist organizations which worked in the years 1968 to 2006; the researchers sifted out 244 organizations that remain active and 136 organizations that have split because it was not possible to know whether their operatives continued to engage in terrorism under a different name and whether the government had defeated them. At this point, the investigators analyzed 268 terrorist organizations that had completely ceased their activities. The researchers found that 43% of terrorist organizations have stopped the activity after political process, that means resolution of the conflict by diplomacy or due to a decision to let down their arms and keep only legitimate political activity. 40% of terrorist organizations have completed their activities due to police and intelligence agencies (like the FBI in the United States). In 7% of cases the government managed to suppress the Organization of terrorism through military means when large military forces sent to fight the terrorist organization. The latter category was the victory of organized terrorism, namely the achievement of the objectives of political strategies.

The findings point that 47% of terrorist organizations did not survive because the army, police forces and the intelligence agencies of the state acted against them and destroyed their spine of command and their operational arms. That is, about half of the terrorist organizations were violently suppressed by the state.[270] The implication of these findings is that about half of the terrorist organizations were defeated and even destroyed, hence the statement that it is impossible to defeat terrorism has no grip on reality.

These findings can be corroborated by many studies that did not directly address the analysis of terrorist organizations but analyzed related or similar phenomena. A country is more likely to win an uprising in countries with strong military power compared to countries without strong military power.[271] Moreover, when the rebel organizations used terrorism in civil wars the probability that the government won is higher than in cases where the rebel organization did not use terrorism.[272] Another study found that in 49% of cases the government won civil wars.[273] Also from many studies analyzing asymmetric wars or insurrections (wars which one side is a state and the other side is non state organization) came up with similar findings.[274]

Although the myth about the impossibility to win terrorist organizations is refuted, I would like to emphasize that it doesn't mean that a state which fight terrorism should use only violent means. It is advisable to use a variety of means such as: military, intelligence, police, economic, legal, diplomatic and media. For example, the Spanish government defeated the Basque underground (ETA) by force, but at the same time they used some political measures, such as granting autonomy to the Basque province.

In addition, as we saw above, high percentage of terrorist organizations ended their activity after they gave up voluntarily the use of terrorism or resolved the conflict by negotiation. If so, the proven ability of countries to suppress the terrorist organizations by violent means does not eliminate the possibility to solve disputes with terrorist organizations through diplomacy, because we must not forget that fighting costs human lives, money and sometimes has a political cost.

Summary

This chapter examines the degree of success of terrorist organizations in three aspects: the life expectancy of terrorist organizations, their success rate in achieving their strategic political goals and the rate of successful repression by violent means. Most terrorist organizations survive for a very short time, and they fail to fulfill their goals fully. In about half of the cases, the governments succeed in eradicating terrorist organizations by force - police or army. Hence the notion that terrorist organizations are successful and that they cannot be defeated by violent means is merely a myth.

Of course, we cannot conclude that terrorist organizations are "paper tigers", meaning they are a threat that we should not underestimate it. Terrorist organizations affect the daily lives of many people around the world. They can cause tremendous damage, they claim human lives and, in some cases, even win their battle. As a result, however, terrorist organizations are tigers whose "hunting strategy" is unsuccessful and many times they are not predators but rather the prey.

Epilogue

In this book a lot of data was examined, and various theories were presented about the reality of terrorism today. From the findings of the studies, we learn that many times the general perception of terrorism is merely a myth; Sometimes the reality is more complex than one might think, and the discussion on terrorism remains too superficial and simplistic.

Terrorism is a complex phenomenon: it is difficult to define the phenomenon, it is not unique to our days, and it is constantly changing. Perceptions that are taken for granted - poverty necessarily causes terrorism or terrorist attacks today are more global than in the past - are not evidence-based perceptions. So are the perceptions of the natural and historical connection between Islam and terrorism that have no grip on reality. Also, the perception that it is impossible to defeat terrorist organizations is a myth.

The scope of research on terrorism increased considerably after the terrorist attacks of September 11, 2001. It increased so much that in the last decade and a half more articles and books on terrorism have been published than in the thirty years preceding 2001. Moreover, the world of terrorism does not freeze, and it is changing, evolving, and surprising. Hence conclusions and explanations we have today may change in the future, and we may find that they were incorrect or inaccurate. If so, the journey to expose reality, refuting myths and understand the phenomenon of terrorism does not end here, curious developments are expected in the future.

Thank you for purchasing this
book.
It is very important for me to hear
what you think about it.
If you loved this book, please leave
a positive review
and if you don't mail me, it will help
me to improve the book.
<u>mytale4u@gmail.com</u>

Notes

1 George W. Bush, Washington D.C. The National Cathedral, September 14 , 2001. http://www.whitehouse.gov

2Jan. A Scholte, "The Globalization of World Politics" in: John Baylis andSteve Smith (eds.), *The Globalization of World Politics: An Introduction to International Relations*, vol. 2, New York: Oxford University Press,2001, pp. 13-3.

3 Andrew Rojecki, "Media Discourse on Globalization and Terror", *Political Communication*, 22(1) (2005): p. 63.

4 Condoleezza Rice, The White House. June 12, 2003. http://www.whitehouse.gov

5 Quoted in: Paul J. Smith, *The Terrorism Ahead: Confronting Transnational Violence in the Twenty-First Century*, Armonk, NY: M.E. Sharpe, 2008, p. 63.

6 Quoted in: Matti Steinberg, "The Theology and Strategy of 'Al-Qaeda' and 'Global Jihad'", *Keshet Hadasha*, 12 (2005), p. 78.

7 Ayman Al-Zawahiri, "Knights under the Prophet's Banner", *A Shark Al-Awsat*, 12 December 2001.

8 Audrey Kurth Cronin, "Behind the Curve: Globalization and International Terrorism", *International Security* 27(3) (2003): 30-58.

9 Ihekwoaba D Onwudiwe, *The Globalization of Terrorism*, Aldershot: Ashgate, 2001.

10Jamal R. Nassar, *Globalization and Terrorism: The Migration of Dreams and Nightmares*, Lanham, MD: Rowman and Littlefield, 2005.

[11] John Mackinlay, "Globalization and Insurgency", London and New York: Routledge, 2002; Harm de Blij, *Why Geography Matters: Three Challenges Facing America: Climate Change, the Rise of China, and Global Terrorism*, Oxford and New York: Oxford University Press, 2005.

[12] Michael. Mousseau, "Market Civilization and Its Clash with Terror", *International Security* 27(3)(2003): 5-29.

[13] Mark Sedgwick, "Inspiration and the Origins of Global Waves of Terrorism", *Studies in Conflict and Terrorism* 30 (2007): 97-112.

[14] Donald Black, "The Geometry of Terrorism", *Sociological Theory* 22(1)80 (2004): 14-25.

[15] Ogen Goldman, "The Globalization of Terrorist Attacks ", *Terrorism and Political Violence* 23(1) (2011): p. 31.

[16] Rapoport, "The Fourth Wave: September 11 in the History of Terrorism".

[17] Martha Crenshaw, "Why America? The Globalization of Civil War", 83 *Current History* 100 (650) (2001): 425-432.

[18] Emmanuel Sivan, *Clash within Islam*, Tel-Aviv: Am-Oved, 2005.

[19] "Saudi Dissident Reportedly Calls for War on U.S. Troops", *Washington Post*, 1996, https://www.washingtonpost.com.

[20] Matti Steinberg, "The Theology and Strategy of Al-Qaeda and Global Jihad", p. 77.

[21] Walter Enders and Todd Sandler, "Is It A Different Now?", *Journal of Conflict Resolution* 49(2) (2005): 259.

[22] To present all measures on the same figure they were calculated as in which every data presents the relative share of all data for the years 1970-2007.

23 Quan Li and Drew Schaub, "Economic Globalization and Transnational Terrorism: A Pooled Time-Series Analysis", *Journal of Conflict Resolution* 48(2) (2004): 230-258.

24 Goldman, "The Globalization of Terrorist Attacks ".

25 Brock S. Blomberg and Gregory D. Hess, "The Lexus and the Olive Branch: Globalization, Democratization and Terrorism", *Terrorism, Economic Development, and Political Openness*, (2008): 116-147.

26 Justin V. Hastings, "Geography, Globalization, and Terrorism: The Plots of Jemaah Islamiyah", *Security Studies* 17(3) (2008): 505-530.

27 Bryan Lowell and Diana Farrel, *Market Unbound: Unleashing Global Capitalism*, New York: John Wiley, 1996; Thomas L. Friedman, *The World Is Flat: A Brief History of the Twenty-First Century*, 1st ed., New York: Farrar, Straus and Giroux, 2005.

28 World Bank, "World Development Indicators", 2008.

29 Yoram Shwatzer and Sari Goldshtein-Farber, "Al Qaeda and the Globalization of Suicide Terrorism"; Moghadam, *The Globalization of Martyrdom*.

30 United Nations, "Terrorism Must Be Adressed in Parralel With Poverty, Underdevelopment, Inequality, General Assembly Told, As General Debate Concluds", 16 November, 2001. https://www.un.org

31 World Bank, 24 Sep. 2018. http://www.worldbank.org.

32 For extended discussion about measuring the poverty line: Ruby Nathanzon, Roy Levi and Amit Leventhal, "International Comparison of Poverty Lines and Selected Tools for Reducing Poverty", *Macro Center for Political Economy*, 2013.

[33] Mark Twain, *The Prince and the Pauper* (Courier Corporation, 2012), 2.

[34] David Gordon, "Indicators of Poverty & Hunger", Expert Group Meeting on Youth Development Indicators (2005): 12-14

[35] Ali Waked, "If the Government of Hamas Will Fall - A Second Somalia Will be Established" YNET, April 16, 2006. https://www.ynet.co.il/articles/0,7340,L-3239274,00.html.

[36] Dany Rubinshtein, "Palestinian Economy: What is Between Poverty and Terrorism?", KalKalist, 30, April 2012. http://www.calcalist.co.il

[37] Andreas Freytag et al., "The Origins of Terrorism: Cross-Country 106 Estimates of Socio-Economic Determinants of Terrorism", *European Journal of Political Economy* 27 (2011): S5-S16.

[38] James A. Piazza, "Incubators of Terror: Do Failed and Failing States Promote Transnational Terrorism?", *International Studies Quarterly* 52(3) (2008): 469-488.

[39] James D. Fearon and David D. Laitin, "Ethnicity, Insurgency, and Civil War", *The American Political Science Review*, 1 (2003):75.

[40] Ted Gurr, *Why Men Rebel*, Princeton: Princeton University Press, 1970.

[41] Martha Crenshaw, "The Causes of Terrorism," *Comparative Politics* 13(4) (1981): 379-399.

[42] Most of the academic literature about the relations between poverty and terrorism focused on the question does poverty influence on the number of terrorist attacks? This chapter is also focused on that specific question. However, poverty is related also to the quality of terrorist attacks (i.e., the number of victims). From several studies it seems that the answer is yes poor economic conditions are related to more lethal terrorist attacks. Efraim Benmelech, Claude Berrebi, and Esteban F. Klor, "Economic

Conditions and the Quality of Suicide Terrorism", *The Journal of Politics* 74 (01) (2012): 113-128; Ethan Bueno De Mesquita, "The Quality of Terror", *American Journal of Political Science* 49(3) (2005): 515-530; Paul Collier and Anke Hoeffler, "Greed and Grievance in Civil War", 56 (2004): 563-595; James D. Fearon and David D. Laitin, "Ethnicity, Insurgency, and Civil War", *American Political Science Review* 97(1) (2003): 75-90; Wayne Nafziger, and Juha Auvinen, "Economic Development, Inequality, War, and State Violence", *World Development* 153-163 :(2002) (2)30.

[43] For example: Doron Peskin, "A Terrorist and A Businessman: Whether Bin-Laden Was A Billionaire or Had only Few Millions? Calcalist, 2, May 2011. https://www.calcalist.co.il

[44] In another study which examined economically developed countries in western Europe a negative statistical relation was found between the number of terrorist attacks and GDP per capita, meaning as the GDP per capita is higher the number of terrorist attacks is lower:

Raul Caruso and Friedrich Schneider, "The Socio-Economic Determinants of Terrorism and Political Violence in Western Europe (1994-2007)", *European Journal of Political Economy* 27 (2011): S37-S49.

Similar findings emerged when all Euro-Asia was analyzed: Santos Bela Ana Bravo and Carlos Manuel Mendes Dias, "An Empirical Analysis of Terrorism: Deprivation, Islamism and Geopolitical Factors", *Defense and Peace Economics* 17(4) (2006): 329-341.

Also form comparative analysis of districts in Turkey:

Kadir Akyuz and Todd Armstrong "Understanding the Socio Structural Correlates of Terrorism in Turkey," *International Criminal Justice Review* 21(2) (2011): 134-155.

In addition, when poverty was measured by consuming per capita (not GDP per capita) it was found that poverty is related to terrorism:

Freytag et al., "The Origins of Terrorism." *European Journal of Political Economy* 27 (2011): s5-s16.

Countries which invest more in welfare suffer less from terrorist attacks that are perpetrated by their citizens in their territory:

Brian Burgoon, "On Welfare and Terror Social Welfare Policies and Political-Economic Roots of Terrorism", *Journal of Conflict Resolution* (2)50 (2006): 176-203.

Richer countries export less terrorists relative to porer countries and citizens of richer countries are more exposed from poorer countries to trans-national terrorist attacks.

Brock Blomberg and Gregory D. Hess, "The Lexus and the Olive Branch: Globalization, Democratization and Terrorism", in: Philip Keefer and Norman Loayza (eds.), *Terrorism, Economic Development, and Political Openness*, New York: Cambridge University Press, 2008, pp. 116-147.

[45] Li and Schaub, "Economic Globalization and Transnational Terrorism".

[46] Li and Schaub.

[47] Caruso and Schneider, "The Socio-Economic Determinants of Western Europe 1994-2007".

[48] Goldman, Shlomo O., and Smadar Noy. 2020. "The Size of Terrorist organizations: Poverty and Economic Inequality as Mobilizing Forces." *Studies in Conflict & Terrorism.* https://doi.org/10.1080/1057610X.2020.1711605.

[49] Tim Krieger and Daniel Meierrieks, "Does Income Inequality Lead to Terrorism". Available at SSRN 1647178, 2010 https://www.econstor.eu.

[50] James A. Piazza, "Poverty, Minority Economic Discrimination, and 118 Domestic Terrorism", *Journal of Peace Research* 48(3) (2011): 339-353.

[51] For literature review about the causes of terrorism:

Meierrieks, "What Causes Terrorism?", *Public Choice* 147(1-2) (2011): 3-27.

[52] Meta-analysis is a method which compare results from many quantitative studies.

[53] Gassebner and Luechinger, "Lock, Stock, and Barrel".

[54] Dipak K. Gupta, *Understanding Terrorism and Political Violence: The Life Cycle of Birth, Growth, Transformation, and Demise*, London and New-York: Routledge, 2008.

[55] James A. Piazza, "Rooted in Poverty? Terrorism, Poor Economic Development, and Social Cleavages", *Terrorism and Political Violence* 18(1) (2006): 159-177.

[56] Alberto Abadie, "Poverty, Political Freedom, and the Roots of Terrorism", *National Bureau of Economic Research*, 2004 http://www.nber.org.

[57] Thomas Gries, Tim Krieger, and Daniel Meierrieks, "Causal Linkages between Domestic Terrorism and Economic Growth", *Defense and Peace Economics* 22(5) (2011): 493-508.

[58] James A. Piazza, "Economic Development, Poorly Managed Political Conflict and Terrorism in India", *Studies in Conflict and Terrorism* 32(5) (2009): 406-419.

[59] James A. Piazza, "Poverty Is Weak Casual Link", in: Stuart Gottlieb (ed.) Debating Terrorism and *Counterterrorism*, Washington D.C: SAGE, 2010, pp. 37-51.

[60] Piazza.

[61] Robert P. Clark, "Patterns in the Lives of ETA Members", *Terrorism* 6(3) 129 (1983): 423-454.

[62] Leonard Weinberg and William Lee Eubank, "Italian Women Terrorists", *Terrorism* 9(3) (1987): 241-262.

[63] Charles A. Russell and Bowman H. Miller, "Profile of a Terrorist", *Terrorism* 1(1) (1977): 17-34.

[64] Marc Sageman, *Understanding Terror Networks*, University of Pennsylvania Press, 2004.

[65] Michael Mousseau, "Urban Poverty and Support for Islamist Terror 133 Survey Results of Muslims in Fourteen Countries", *Journal of Peace Research* 48(1) (2011): 35-47.

[66] Alan B. Krueger and Jitka Malecková, "Education, Poverty and Terrorism: Is There a Causal Connection?", *The Journal of Economic Perspectives* 17 (2003): 119-144.

[67] Actually, they found a reverse relation between poverty and recruitment to the armed wing of Hezbollah. Meaning, as someone was poorer the probability that he would be recruited to Hezbollah was lower. However, when they inserted other demographic variables this significant relation was gone.

[68] Jennifer Kavanagh, "Selection, Availability, and Opportunity: The Conditional Effect of Poverty on Terrorist Group Participation", *Journal of Conflict Resolution* (2011): 1 55, 106-132.

Similar findings emerged in a study about the resistant movement to the British rule in Bengal in the beginning of the 20th century. This study pointed out that the political activists, violent and nonviolent ones, were richer and more educated than the rest of the population. However, the violent political activists relative to the nonviolent activists, tend to belong to the lower parts of society but only among the educated ones.

Alexander Lee, "Who Becomes a Terrorist? Poverty, Education, and the Origins of Political Violence", *World Politics* 63(2) (2011): 203-245.

[69] Alan B Krueger and David Laitin, "Kto Koto?: A Cross-Country Study of Origins and Targets of Terrorism", in: Philip Keefer and Norman Loayza (eds.), *Terrorism, Economic Development, and Political Openness* New- York: Cambridge University Press, 2008, pp. 148-173.

[70] Claude Berrebi, "Evidence about the Link between Education, Poverty and Terrorism among Palestinians", *Peace Economics, Peace Science and Public Policy* 13(1) (2007): 1-36. http://www.degruyter.com

[71] Brian Lai, "Draining the Swamp: An Empirical Examination of the Production of International Terrorism, 1968-1998", *Conflict Management and Peace Science* 24(4) (2007): 297-310.

[72] Piazza, "Poverty, Minority Economic Discrimination, and Domestic Terrorism".

[73] Walter Enders and Gary A. Hoover, "The Nonlinear Relationship between Terrorism and Poverty", *The American Economic Review* 102(3) (2012): 267-272; Walter Enders, Gary A. Hoover, and Todd Sandler, "The Changing Nonlinear Relationship between Income and Terrorism", *Journal of Conflict Resolution* 6(2) (2016): 195-225.

[74] Other scholars also found the non-linear relations between poverty and terrorism:

Brock S. Blomberg and Gregory D. Hess, "From (No) Butter to Guns? Understanding the Economic Role in Transnational Terrorism", *Terrorism, Economic Development, and Political Openness*, 2008, 83-115; Krisztina Kis-Katos, Helge Liebert, and Günther G. Schulze, "On the Origin of Domestic and International Terrorism", *European Journal of Political Economy* 27 (2011): S17 S36; Lai, *"Draining the Swamp': An Empirical Examination of the Production of International Terrorism, 1968-1998"*.

[75] Ariel Chana, "Sweden wears Kaffiyah and Israel is apathic", Ma'ariv 8, October 2014. NRG, https://www.makorrishon.co.il.

[76] Israel Rosen, "Only Jewish Nation State Can Cope with Terrorism", Shabth Be'Shabato, 1551, 29 November 2014. https://www.zomet.org.il

[77] Victor Asal and Andrew Blum, "Holy Terror and Mass Killings? Reexamining the Motivations and Methods of Mass Casualty Terrorists", *International Studies Review* 7(1) (2005): 153-155.

[78] The review about the Thugs is based on:

David Rapoport, "Fear and Trembling: Terrorism in Three Religious Traditions", *American Political Science Review* 78(3) (1984): 658-677.

[79] Mark Juergensmeyer, *Global Rebellion: Religious Challenges to the Secular State, from Christian Militias to Al Qaeda,* Berkley: University of California Press, 2008; Mark Juergensmeyer, *Terror in the Mind of God: The Global Rise of Religious Violence,* Berkeley, California: University of California Press, 2000; Mark Juergensmeyer, "Religion as a Root Cause of Terrorism", in: Louise Richardson (ed.), *The Roots of Terrorism*, London: Routledge, Taylor and Francis Group, 2006, pp. 133-143.

[80] Jeffrey R Seul, "Ours Is the Way of God?: Religion, Identity, and Intergroup Conflict", *Journal of Peace Research* 36(5) (1999): 553-569; Jonathan Fox, "Religious Causes of Discrimination against Ethno-

Religious Minorities", *International Studies Quarterly* 44(3) (2000): 423-450; Jonathan Fox, *Religion, Civilization, and Civil War: 1945 through the Millennium*, Lanham, MD: Lexington Books, 2004.

[81]Nilay Saiya and Anthony Scime, "Explaining Religious Terrorism: A Data-Mined Analysis", *Conflict Management and Peace Science* 32(5) (2015): 487-512.

[82] Nil Satana, Molly Inman, and Johanna Kristin Birnir, "Religion, Government Coalitions and Terrorism", *Terrorism and Political Violence* 25(1) (2013): 29-52; Juergensmeyer, *Terror in the Mind of God: The Global Rise of Religious Violence*, University of California Press ,2007.

[83] Jonathan Fox, "Do Religious Institutions Support Violence or the Status Quo?", *Studies in Conflict and Terrorism* 22(2) (1999): 119-139; Mohammed M Hafz, *Why Muslims Rebel: Repression and Resistance in the Islamic World*, Boulder, CO: Lynne Rienner, 2003; Brain Grim and Roger Finke, The *Price of Freedom Denied: Religious Persecution and Conflict in the Twenty First Century*, New York: Cambridge University Press, 2011.

[84]Emile Sahliyeh, *Religious Resurgence and Politics in the Contemporary World*, New York: State University of New York Press, 1990.

[85]Sam Harris, *The End of Faith: Religion, Terror, and the Future of Reason*, London: Norton & Company, 2004, esp. p. 19.

[86] Jonathan Fox, "The Religious Wave: Religion and Domestic Conflict from 1960 to 2009", *Civil Wars* 14(2) (2012): 141-158.

[87] Samuel P. Huntington, "The Clash of Civilizations?", *Foreign Affairs* 72(3) (1993): 22-49.

[88] One of the reasons is the fall of the Soviet Union and the rapid changes in the international system. Because of these changes religion has became a stable part in the turmoil of international affairs. Moreover, few nations declined both the Communist and

the American perceptions because they wanted to establish their own nationality, which based on their own cultural and religious roots. In addition, the big ideologies (Capitalism, Liberalism and Communism) failed many around the world because they did not bring prosperity to third world countries. By contrast the religion does not promise material reward in this world therefore cannot let down in the economic sense. Last, there was a filling that the secular governments round the world failed in defending on unique communities and their national culture. Moreover, many of these regimes were even suppressive and harmed the religious or national identities therefore hurt the pride of many believers.

Mark Juergensmeyer, *The New Cold War*, California: University of California Press, 1993; Juergensmeyer, *Global Rebellion: Religious Challenges to the Secular State, from Christian Militias to Al Qaeda*; Mark Juergensmeyer, "Terror Mandated by God", *Terrorism and Political Violence* 9(2) (1997): 16-23.

[89] Quoted in: Magnus Ranstorp, "Terrorism in the Name of: Religion", *Journal of International Affairs* 50(1) (1996): 41-62.

[90] David C. Rapoport, "Sacred Terror: A Contemporary Example From 158 Islam", in: Walter Reich (ed.), *Origins of Terrorism Psychologies, Ideologies, Theories, States of Mind*, New York: University of Cambridge, 1990, pp. 103-130; David Rapoport, "The Four Waves of Modern Terrorism", in: Audrey Cronin and James Ludes (eds.), *The Campaign Against International Terrorism*, Washington D.C: Georgetown University Press, 2004, pp. 46-73; David C. Rapoport, "The Four Waves of Terror and September 11," *Anthropoetics* 8(1) (2002): online http://anthropoetics.ucla.edu.

Like him, Pestana Barros and Proenca claimed that secular terrorism was replaced by the radical Islamic terrorism because of the Islamic revolution in Iran in 1979 and the Soviet invasion to Afghanistan.

Carlos Pestana Barros and Isabel Proenca, "Mixed Logit Estimation of Radical Islamic Terrorism in Europe and North America: A Comparative Study", *Journal of Conflict Resolution* 49(2) (2005): 298-314.

[91] Rapoport, "The Four Waves of Terror and September 11"; Rapoport, "The Four Waves of Modern Terrorism".

[92] Fox, "The Religious Wave: Religion and Domestic Conflict from 1960 to 2009".

However, there is no consensus about the extent of religious involvement that is needed to consider a conflict as a religious one. Additionally, many times in religious conflicts non religios factors are involved, such as: corruption of the government, bad economic situation and nationality.

Fox; Juergensmeyer, *Global Rebellion: Religious Challenges to the Secular State, from Christian Militias to Al Qaeda.*

[93]Karen Rasler and William R. Thompson, "Looking for Waves of Terrorism", *Terrorism and Political Violence* 21(1) (2009): 28-41.

[94] Rasler and Thompson, p. 35.

[95] Fox claimed that the ending of the Cold War and the fall of the Communist Block encouraged religious conflict, so in 2002 most of domestic conflicts were religious. These findings support mainly Rapoport's wave theory and the claims of Jungermaier, but not Huntington's claims, secularization claims nor the claims about the stability in the role of religious role in our life. Religion, as a root cause of conflicts take central place more than the past and the timing of the rise of religious terrorism fits the claim that the religious terrorism started in the end of the 1970s.

Fox, "The Religious Wave: Religion and Domestic Conflict from 1960 to 2009" Samuel Huntington, "The Clash of Civilizations" Foreign Affairs (1993):72(3) 164, 22-49; Samuel Huntington, *The*

Clash of Civilizations and the Remaking of World Order, New-York: Simon and Schuster, 1996.

[96] Samuel Huntington, "The Clash of Civilizations" *Foreign Affairs* 72(3) 164 (1993): 22-49; Samuel Huntington, *The Clash of Civilizations and the Remaking of World Order*, New-York: Simon and Schuster, 1996.

[97] According to another explanation, which criticized Huntington's arguments, the polarization between McWorld and the Jihad is actually polarization between global consuming Capitalist forces (McWorld) and the tribe cultures which seek to preserve the traditional culture (Jihad). According to this explanation, Huntington's sorting to the traditional civilizations and the argument about the polarization is based on these civilizations and not because Jihad exists also in the Western (Christian) civilization, for example in skinheads, Neo-Nazis, etc.

Barber, Benjamin, *McWorld, vs. Jihad*, New York: Ballantine Books, 1995.

Another critic is focused on Huntington's argument that the main confrontation is between Islam and the West. According to this critic, the main confrontation the main violent conflict is inside Islam, not between Islam and other cultures. Emmanuel Sivan thinks that Huntington was fooled by the rhetoric of small group inside Islam that promotes struggle between Islam and the West, but this group does not present the Islamic civilization; Emmanuel Sivan, *Clash Within Islam*, Am-Oved: Tel-Aviv, 2005.

[98] Fox, *Religion, Civilization, and Civil War: 1945 through the Millennium*, 166, pp. 182, 202-203.

In one study the relations between inter-religious differences to the general rate of domestic violent conflicts during the Cold-War and Post-Cold War. The findings shows that only in the first decade after the Cold-War there was a significant relation between inter-religious differences and violent domestic conflicts.

Tanja Ellingsen,"Toward a Revival of Religion and Religious Clashes?", in: Jonathan Fox and Shmuel Sandler (eds.), Religion in World Conflict, Routledge: London, 2006, pp.11-38.

Generally, studies which criticized Huntington's theses about the clash of civilizations pointed out that there is no empirical evidence to suggest differences between the Cold-War and Post-Cold-War era in inter-cultural clashes.

[99] Fox, Religion, *Civilization, and Civil War: 1945 through the Millennium*, pp. 176.

[100] Fox, "The Religious Wave: Religion and Domestic Conflict from 1960 to 2009".

[101] For example: Errol A Henderson, "Mistaken Identity: Testing the Clash of Civilizations Thesis in Light of Democratic Peace Claims", *British Journal of Political Science* 34(3) (2004): 539-554; Steven Fish and Francesca Jensenius, "Islam and Large-Scale Political Violence: Is There

a Connection?", *Comparative Political Studies* 43(11) (2010): 1327-1362; Sean Bolks and Richard Stoll, "Examining Conflict Escalation Within the Civilizational Context", *Conflict Management and Peace Science* 20(1) (2003):85-109; Bruce M. Russet, John R. Oneal, and Michaelene Cox, "Clash of Civilizations, or Realism and Liberalism Deja Vu? Some Evidence", *Journal of Peace Research* 37, 5 (2000): 583-608; Giacomo Chiozza, "Is There a Clash of Civilizations? Evidence from Patterns of International Conflict Involvement, 1946–97", *Journal of Peace Research* 39(6) (2002): 711-734; Erik Gartzke and Kristian Skrede Gleditsch, "Identity and Conflict: Ties That Bind and Differences That Divide", *European Journal of International Relations* 12(1) (2006): 53-87.

[102]Gabriel Ben-Dor and Ami Pedahzur, "The Uniqueness of Islamic Fundamentalism and the Fourth Wave of International Terrorism", in: Leonard Weinberg and Ami Pedahzur (ed.), *Religious Fundamentalism and Political Extremism*, London: Frank Cass, 2004, pp. 71-91.

[103] Eric Neumayer and Thomas Plumper, "International Terrorism and the Clash of Civilizations," *British Journal of Political Science* 39(4) (2009):711-734.

[104]Emmanuel Sivan, Clash Within Islam, Am-Oved: Tel-Aviv, 2005.

[105] Steinberg, "The Theology and Strategy of Al-Qaeda and Global Jihad".

[106] Kenneth Katzman, "Al Qaeda: Profile and Threat Assessment", CRS, August 17, 2005.

[107] Saudi Dissident Reportedly Calls for War on U.S. Troops", Washington Post, 1996, https://www.washingtonpost.com.

[108]Steinberg, "The Theology and Strategy of Al-Qaeda and Global Jihad", p. 77.

[109] Al-Zawahiri, "Knights Under the Prophet's Banner".

[110] Rapoport, "Fear and Trembling: Terrorism in Three Religious Traditions", p. 672.

[111] Bruce Hoffman, "Terrorism Trends and Prospects", in: Bruce Hoffman et al (eds.), *Countering the New Terrorism*, Santa Monica: RAND Corporation, 1999, pp. 7-38.

[112] Juergensmeyer, *Terror in the Mind of God: The Global Rise of Religious Violence*.

[113] Justin Conrad and Daniel Milton, "Unpacking the Connection between Terror and Islam", *Studies in Conflict and Terrorism* 36(4) (2013): 315-336.

[114] Lawrence R. Iannaccone, "Sacrifice and Stigma: Reducing Free-Riding in Cults, Communes, and Other Collectives", *Journal of Political Economy* 1000 (1992): 271-292; Laurence R. Iannaccone and Eli Berman, "Religious Extremists: The Good, the Bad and the Deadly", *Public Choice* 128 (2006): 109-129; Eli Berman, "Hamas, Taliban, and the Jewish Underground: An Economist's View of Radical Religious Militias", *NBER Working Paper No. W10004* (2003); Eli Berman and David Laitin, "Religion, Terrorism and Public Goods: Testing the Club Model", *Journal of Public Economics* 92 (2008): 1942-1967.

[115] Alon Burstein, "Armies of God, Armies of Men: A Global Comparison of Secular and Religious Terror Organizations", *Terrorism and Political Violence* 30 (2018): 1-21.

[116] Asal and Blum, "Holy Terror and Mass Killings? Reexamining the Motivations and Methods of Mass Casualty Terrorists," p. 154.

[117] James A. Piazza, "Is Islamist Terrorism More Dangerous? An Empirical Study of Group Ideology, Organization, and Goal Structure", *Terrorism and Political Violence* 21 (2009): 62-88.

[118] Mia M. Bloom, *Dying to Kill: The Global Phenomenon of Suicide Terror*, New York: Columbia University Press, 2004.

[119] Walter Enders and Todd Sandler, "Is Transnational Terrorism Becoming More Threatening?: A Time-Series Investigation", *Journal of Conflict Resolution* 44(3) (2000): 307-332.

[120] Piazza, "Is Islamist Terrorism More Dangerous?: An Empirical Study of Group Ideology,

Jessica Stern, Terror in the Name of God, New York: HarperCollins, 2003.

[121] Ranstorp, "Terrorism in the Name of Religion", p. 54.

Stern claimed that these are the organizations which most likely would use weapons of mass destruction. Jessica Stern, *Terror in the Name of God*, New York: HarperCollins, 2003, p. xxii

[122] Bruce Hoffman, "'Holy Terror': The Implications of Terrorism 191 Motivated by A Religious Imperative", *RAND Corporation*, 1993, pp.2-3; Hoffman, *Inside Terrorism*, 1998, pp. 94-95.

[123] Cronin, "Behind the Curve," pp. 41-42.

[124] For example: Victor Asal and Karl Rethemeyr, "The Nature of the Beast: Organizational Structures and the Lethality of Terrorist Attacks", *Journal of Politics* 70(2) (2008): 437-449; Assaf Moghadam, "Motives for Martyrdom: Al-Qaida, Salafi Jihad, and the Spread of Suicide Attacks", *International Security* 33(3) (2008): 46-78.

[125] Asal and Blum, "Holy Terror and Mass Killings? Reexamining the Motivations and Methods of Mass Casualty Terrorists"; Piazza, "Is Islamist Terrorism More Dangerous?: An Empirical Study of Group Ideology, Organization, and Goal Structure"; Alon Burstein, "Armies of God, Armies of Men: A Global Comparison of Secular and Religious Terror Organizations".

[126] Asal and Rethemeyr, "The Nature of the Beast: Organizational Structures and the Lethality of Terrorist Attacks"; Daniel Masters, "The Origin of Terrorist Threats: Religious, Separatist, or Something Else?", *Terrorism and Political Violence* 20(3) (2008): 396-414.

[127] Susanna Pearce, "Religious Rage: A Quantitative Analysis of the Intensity of Religious Conflicts", *Terrorism and Political Violence* 17(3) (2005):333-352.

[128] Bernard Lewis, "The Roots of Muslim Rage," *The Atlantic* 266(3) (1990): 47-60.

[129] Mia M. Bloom, *Dying to Kill: The Allure of Suicide Terror*, New York: Clumbia University Press, 2005, p. 133; Robert Anthony

Pape, *Dying to Win: The Strategic Logic of Suicide Terrorism*, New-York: Random House, 2005.

130 Bloom, *Dying to Kill: The Global Phenomenon of Suicide Terror,* Pape, *Dying to Win.*

131 Walter Laqueur, *No End to War: Terrorism in the Twenty-First Century*, New York: Continuum, 2003, p.78.

132 Audrey Kurth Cronin, "Terrorists and Suicide Attacks", *CRS*, August 23, 2003. https://fas.org/irp/crs/RL32058.pdf

133 Cronin.

134 Peter Henne, "The Ancient Fire: Religion and Suicide Terrorism," *Terrorism and Political Violence* 24 (2012): 38-60.

135 Quoted in: Conrad and Milton, "Unpacking the Connection between Terror and Islam".

136 Richard Jackson, "Constructing Enemies: 'Islamic Terrorism' in Political and Academic Discourse", Government and Opposition 42(3) (2007): 394-426.

137Barak Mendelsohn, "Sovereignty under Attack: The International Society Meets the Al Qaeda Network", Review of International Studies 31(1) (2005): 55-57.

138 Lewis, "The Roots of Muslim Rage".

139 Stern, *Terror in the Name of God*, pp. 264, 281, 286-287.

140 Scott Atran, *Talking to the Enemy: Religion, Brotherhood, and the (Un) Making of Terrorists*, New York: Ecco/HarperCollins, 2010.

141 Jackson, "Constructing Enemies: 'Islamic Terrorism' in Political and Academic Discourse".

142 Walter Laqueur, *The New Terrorism: Fanaticism and the Arms of Mass Destruction*, New York: Oxford University Press, 1999, pp. 127-129.

[143] Until the Islamic Revolution in Iran, no suicide bombings took place. Shortly afterwards, suicide bombings began in the Iran-Iraq War and Lebanon. Iran's envoys have been working in Lebanon since 1982 to market the Islamic Revolution. Shortly afterwards, suicide bombings began in Lebanon. The largest was carried out against the multinational American and French forces; there were hundreds killed. It should be noted that while suicide is forbidden under Islam, suicide bombings are different. Some Muslim jurists and leaders of Islamic terrorist organizations see them as having died for Allah and not as suicides. Unlike a person who harms himself due to personal despair, a man who kills others in the service of Islam dies a martyr.

A. J Caschetta, "Does Islam Have a Role in Suicide Bombings?", *Middle East Quarterly* 22(3) (2015): 1-19; Matthew Levitt, *Hezbollah, The Global Footprint of Lebanon's Party of God*, Washington, D.C: Georgetown University Press, 2013, p. 12.

[144] Juergensmeyer, *Terror in the Mind of God: The Global Rise of Religious Violence*; Rapoport, "The Four Waves of Terror and September 11"; Scott Atran, "The Genesis of Suicide Terrorism," Science 299 (2003):1534-1539.

[145] Hoffman, *Inside Terrorism*, 1998, pp. 93-94.

[146] Hoffman, "Terrorism Trends and Prospects".

[147] Conrad and Milton, "Unpacking the Connection between Terror and Islam".

[148] Piazza, "Is Islamist Terrorism More Dangerous?: An Empirical Study of Group Ideology, Organization, and Goal Structure", p. 64.

[149] Sara Jackson Wade and Dan Reiter, "Does Democracy Matter? Regime Type and Suicide Terrorism", *Journal of Conflict Resolution* 51(2) (2007): 329-348; Piazza, "Is Islamist Terrorism More

Dangerous?: An Empirical Study of Group Ideology, Organization, and Goal Structure".

[150] John L. Esposito, *Unholy War: Terror in the Name of Islam*, Oxford: Open University Press, 2006; Lewis Bernard, *The Crisis of Islam: Holy War and Unholy Terror*, New York: Modern Library, 2003.

[151] Piazza, "Is Islamist Terrorism More Dangerous?: An Empirical Study of Group Ideology, Organization, and Goal Structure". Source: *Terrorism knowledge base* (www.tkb.org).

[152] According to an alternative explanation the terrorists belong to a variety of religions, hence the connection between suicide terrorism to Islam is minimal.

Pape, *Dying to Win*, p. 4.

The data presented in this study are biased, as Japanese kamikaze pilots were also included in the analysis, and so the numbers were skewed in favor of the claim that there is no connection between suicide terrorism and Islam. However, the kamikaze phenomenon in World War II does not belong to the phenomenon of suicide terrorism: Japanese suicide bombers represented a country, they flew planes marked with a Japanese symbol and attacked only military targets in wartime. Moreover, out of 18 cases of suicide the researcher counted, including cases that at the time of writing the study were not yet complete, 12 of which were carried out by Islamic terrorist organizations. Moreover, most of the organizations in the study are Islamic (also the Chechens and Iraqis who are not named). Therefore, it is not clear why the researcher concluded that Islam is not related to suicide terrorism.

Caschetta, "Does Islam Have a Role in Suicide Bombings?"

[153] Piazza, "Is Islamist Terrorism More Dangerous?:An Empirical Study of Group Ideology, Organization, and Goal Structure";

James A. Piazza, "A Supply-Side View of Suicide Terrorism: A Cross-National Study," *The Journal of Politics* 70(1) (2008): 28-39.

[154] Bruce Hoffman and Gordon H. McCormick, "Terrorism, Signaling, and Suicide Attack", *Studies in Conflict and Terrorism* 27(4): 243-281.

[155] Palestinian Media Watch, Hamas Leader: We Love Death as Our Enemy [Israel] Love Life, 30 Julay, 2014.

http://www.palwatch.org.il

[156] Cronin, "Terrorists and Suicide Attacks"; Boaz Ganor, "Suicide Atacks in Israel", in: *Countering Suicide Terrorism* Herzliya: International Institute for Counter Terrorism, 2002.

[157] Cronin, "Terrorists and Suicide Attacks", p. 3.

[158] Cronin, "Terrorists and Suicide Attacks" p. 4 227.

[159] Ehud Sprinzak, "Rational Fanatics", *Foreign Policy*, 120 (2000): 66-73.

[160] National Consortium for the Study of Terrorism and Responses to Terrorism (START), "Global Terrorism Database [Data File]", 2013 http://www.start.umd.edu.

[161] Cronin, "Terrorists and Suicide Attacks"

[162] Martha Crenshaw, "Suicide Terrorism in Comparative Perspective", in: *Countering Suicide Terrorism: An International Conference* (Herzelia: The International Policy Institute for Counterterrorism, 2001), p. 28.

[163] Cronin, "Terrorists and Suicide Attacks".

[164] Mia M. Bloom, "Palestinian Suicide Bombing: Public Support, Market Share, and Outbidding", *Political Science Quarterly* 119(1) (2004): 61-88.

165 Dipak K. Gupta and Kusum Mundra, "Suicide Bombing as a Strategic Weapon: An Empirical Investigation of Hamas and Islamic Jihad" *Terrorism and Political Violence* 17(4) (2005): 573-598.

166PEW Research Center, *Muslim Publics Share Concerns about Extremist Groups*. http://www.pewglobal.org

167 Chicago Project on Security and Threats (CPOST). 2018. *Suicide Attack Database September 2018 Release.* Retrieved from http://cpost.uchicago.edu.

168 Chicago Project on Security and Terrorism (CPOST). 2016. *Suicide Attack Database* (October 12, 2016, Release). [Data File] http://cpostdata.uchicago.edu.

169 Benjamin Acosta and Steven J. Childs, "Illuminating the Global Suicide- 237 Attack Network", *Studies in Conflict and Terrorism* 36(1) (2013): 49-76.

170 Moghadam, The Globalization of Martyrdom.

171 Schwayzer and Goldstein-Farber, Al-Qaeda and the Globalization of Suicide Terrorism, p. 33.

172 Yoram Schwayzer, "The Perception of Istishad and its Proliferation by Al-Qaeda" in: Shaul Shay and Hagai Erlich (Eds.) Ticking Bomb: The Suicide Terrorists and The Coping with Them", Tel-Aviv: Maarachot, 2006' pp. 217-230.

173 Yizhak Ben-Israel, "Coping with Suicide Terrorism – the Israeli Case", in: Shaul Shay and Haggai Golan (Eds.), Ticking Bomb: The Suicide Terrorists and The Coping with Them, Tel-Aviv: Ma'arachot, 2006, p. 39.

174 Pape, Dying to Win, pp. 20-23

175 Benjamin Acosta, "Suicide-Attack Network Database", *Claremont LION Initiative,* January 1, 2014. http://www.claremontlion.org.

[176] Wade and Reiter, "Does Democracy Matter?" *Regime Type and Suicide Terrorism.*

[177] Piazza, "A Supply-Side View of Suicide Terrorism".

[178] Assaf Moghadam, "Suicide Terrorism, Occupation, and the Globalization of Martyrdom: A Critique of Dying to Win", *Studies in Conflict and Terrorism* 29(8) (2006): 707-729.

[179] Scott Atran, "Trends in Suicide Terrorism: Sense and Nonsense", 2004, p. 248-5. http://www.artisresearch.com

[180] Adam Lankford, "Could Suicide Terrorists Actually Be Suicidal?", *Studies in Conflict and Terrorism* 34(4) (2011): 337-366.

[181] Luis de la Corte Ibáñez, "The Social Psychology of Suicide Terrorism" (International Institute for Counter Terrorism, October 2014).

[182] Sprinzak, "Rational Fanatics".

[183] Anat Berko, Bomb Women: Suicide Terrorists – Women and Children in the Service of Terror, Tel-Aviv: Yediot Aharonot Sifrey Hemed, 2010, p. 19 .

[184] Crenshaw, "Suicide Terrorism in Comparative Perspective", p. 25.

[185] Crenshaw, p. 26.

[186] De la Corte Ibáñez, "The Social Psychology of Suicide Terrorism".

[187] Bruce Hoffman and Gordon H. McCormick, "Terrorism, Signaling, and 256 Suicide Attack", *Studies in Conflict and Terrorism* 27(4) (2004): 243-281.

[188] Scott Atran, "The Moral Logic and Growth of Suicide Terrorism", *Washington Quarterly* 29(2) (2006): 127-147; Bloom, *Dying to Kill: The Allure of Suicide Terror.*

[189] The Attack (L'Attentat), translated by John Cullen (Nan A. Talese, 2006).

[190] Boaz Ganor, "Suicide Terrorism: An Overview, Who Is the Shahid?", Herzelia: International Policy Institute for Counter-Terrorism, p. 3.

[191] Niall Ferguson, Civilization: The West and the Rest, London: Pinguin Books, 2011.

[192] Cronin, "Terrorists and Suicide Attacks".

[193] The Sociology and Psychology of Terrorism", Washington, D.C: *Federal Research Division Library of Congress*, September 1999, p. 40.

[194] Ariel Merari, "Social, Organizational and Psychologicl Factors in Suicide Terrorism", in: Tore Bjorgo (ed.), *Root Causes of Terrorism: Myths, Reality and Ways Forward* Abington: Routledge, 2004, pp. 70-86.

[195] Sprinzak, "Rational Fanatics".

[196] The calculation is based on data from: *Chicago Project on Security and Terrorism (CPOST)*, "Suicide Attack Database", October 12, 2016.

[197] Debra D. Zedalis, "Female Suicide Bombers", The Minerva Group, Inc., 2004.

[198] Berrebi, "Evidence About the Link between Education, Poverty and Terrorism Among Palestinians".

[199] Ami Pedahzur, Arie Perliger, and Leonard Weinberg, "Altruism and Fatalism: The Characteristics of Palestinian Suicide Terrorists", *Deviant Behavior* 24(4) (2003): 405-423.

[200] Assaf Moghadam, "Palestinian Suicide Terrorism in the Second Intifada: Motivations and Organizational Aspects", *Studies in Conflict and Terrorism* 26(2) (2003): 65-92.

[201]Benmelech, Berrebi, and Klor, "Economic Conditions and the Quality of Suicide Terrorism".

[202] Anat Berko, *Bomb Women: Suicide Terrorists – Women and Children in the Service of Terror*, p. 182-183.

[203] Moghadam, "Palestinian Suicide Terrorism in the Second Intifada".

[204] Atran, "Trends in Suicide Terrorism," p. 7.

[205] Atran, p. 10.

[206] Anat Berko, *Bomb Women: Suicide Terrorists – Women and Children in the Service of Terror*, p. 185.

[207] De la Corte Ibáñez, "The Social Psycology of Suicide Terrorism".

[208] Ami Pedahzur and Arie Prelinger, "The Factors which Explain the Emergence of Suicide Terrorism: Three-Dimensional Model", in: Shaul Shay and Haggai Golan (Eds.), *Ticking Bomb: The Suicide Terrorists and The Coping with Them*, Tel-Aviv: Ma'arachot, 2006, pp. 47-61.

[209] The comparison period 2004-2000 was chosen because these were the peak years of the second intifada. This was followed by a dramatic drop in the rate of attacks and in the rate of casualties. In the following five years, January-2005 December 2009 another 150 people were murdered. The rate of victims in the decade since the beginning of the second intifada was four times higher than the rate of victims in the eleven years before the outbreak the Intifada.

[210] Israeli General Security Service, Distribution of Victims from Palestinian Terrorism in the Present Confrontation, 29 September 2000-31 December 2009. https://www.shabak.gov.il.

[211] Aaron Levran, "No Steril Wars", Haaretz, 27 October 2003. https://www.haaretz.co.il

212 "General Samia: "the Slogan 'Let IDF Win' Is vices", YNET 18 December 2014, https://www.ynet.co.il.

213 Quoted in: Zaki Shalom and Yoaz Hendel, Let the IDF Win, Tel-Aviv: Yediot Aharonot, 2010, p. 42.

214 Sharon Sade, "The European Armies, Says Secretary General of NATO, are Depleted and Soft Gaint", Haaretz, 23 October 2002. https://www.haaretz.co.il

215Flavius, Josephus. "Wars of the Jews." Whiston W.(transl.) The Complete Works of Josephus: Kregel Publications, Grand Rapids, Michigan, Book 7 1995.

216 Flavius, Josephus "Wars of the Jews".

217 Max Abrahms, "The Political Effectiveness of Terrorism Revisited", *Comparative Political Studies* 45(3) (2012): 366-393.

218 Ron Tira, "The Struggle on the Nature of War: From Clausewitz to Scipio Africanos and Anuar Saadat, till the The State Enemy Which Adapted to the War Against the RMA", ISSN Tel-Aviv: Tel-Aviv University, 2008, p. 71.

219 Tom Dannenbaum, "Bombs, Ballots, and Coercion: The Madrid Bombings, Electoral Politics, and Terrorist Strategy", *Security Studies* 20(3) (2011): 303-349; William Rose, Rysia Murphy, and Max Abrahms, "Does Terrorism Ever Work? The 2004 Madrid Train Bombings", *International Security* 32(1) (2007): 185-192.

220 Martha Crenshaw, "How Terrorism Declines", *Terrorism and Political Violence* 3(1) (1991): 69-87; Peter Krause, "The Political Effectiveness of Non-State Violence: A Two-Level Framework to Transform a Deceptive Debate", *Security Studies* 22(2) (2013): 259-294.

221 Paul Wilkinson, *Terrorism versus Democracy: The Liberal State Response*, Taylor & Francis, 2006, p. 6.

[222] Gupta, *Understanding Terrorism and Political Violence*, pp. 187-188.

[223] Walter Laqueur, "Left, Right and Beyond: The Changing Face of Terror", in: James F Hoge and Gideon Rose (eds.), *Understanding the War on Terror*, New York: Council on Foreign Relations, 2005, p. 154.

[224] Wilkinson, *Terrorism versus Democracy*, pp. 22-23.

[225] Gloria G. *Schlaepfer, Butterflies*, New York: Benchmark Books, 2004, pp. 76-77.

[226] Schlaepfer, Butterflies, 76.

[227] Audrey Kurth Cronin, *How Terrorism Ends: Understanding the Decline and Demise of Terrorist Campaigns*, Princeton, N.J: Princeton University Press, 2009, p. 221.

[228] Brock Blomberg, Khusrav Gaibulloev, and Todd Sandler, "Terrorist Group Survival: Ideology, Tactics, and Base of Operations", *Public Choice* 149(3-4) (2011): 441-463.

[229] Khusrav Gaibulloev and Todd Sandler, "Determinants of the Demise of Terrorist Organizations", *Southern Economic Journal* 79(4) (2013): 774-792.

[230] Shlomo Ogen Goldman and Leah Bar, "The Global Law of Terror Organization Lifespan", *Terrorism and Political Violence*, (August 8, 2018).

[231] Ron Jacobs, *The Way the Wind Blew: A History of the Weather Underground*, London and New-York: Verso, 1997; Seth G. Jones and Martin C. Libicki, *How Terrorist Groups End*, Santa Monica, CA: RAND, 2008. http://www.rand.org.

[232] Data was measured annually, so probably 50% of terrorist organizations survived four years or less.

[233] Seth G. Jones and Martin C. Libicki, How Terrorist Groups End, Santa Monica, CA: RAND, 2008. http://www.rand.org.

[234] Cronin did not insert all terrorist organizations that committed one terrorist attacks or simultaneous terrorist attacks, therefore in her study the half lifetime is higher and is eight years.

Audrey Kurth Cronin, *How Terrorism Ends: Understanding the Decline and Demise of Terrorist Campaigns*, Princeton, N.J: Princeton University Press, 2009.

In addition to the study of Blomberg Gaibulloev and Sandler, which were quoted above, I based on these studies: S. Brock Blomberg, Rozlyn C. Engel, and Reid Sawyer, "On the Duration and Sustainability of Transnational Terrorist Organizations", *Journal of Conflict Resolution* 54(2) (2009): 303-330; Brian J. Phillips, "Terrorist Group Cooperation and Longevity", *International Studies Quarterly* 58(2) (2013): 1-12; Joseph K. Young and Laura Dugan, "Survival of the Fittest: Why Terrorist Groups Endure", *Perspectives on Terrorism* 8(2) (2014): 2-23 http://terrorismanalysts.com.

[235] An average of about 11.5 years in the group of terrorist organizations that won, compared with about 7 years of terrorist organizations that did not win. Standard deviation 10.5 and 10.3 respectively p <0.05, T = 2.08. The calculations and the division into organizations that won and did not win was performed according to this database: Seth G. Jones and Martin C. Libicki, *How Terrorist Groups End*, Santa Monica, CA: RAND, 2008.

Like these differences, studies also found differences between organizations that were successful in the rebellion and these that did not: David C. Gompert et al., *War by Other Means — Building Complete and Balanced Capabilities for Counterinsurgency*, Santa Monica, CA: RAND, 2008.

[236]Cronin, How Terrorism Ends, 220.

[237] Mao Tse-Tung, "U.S. Imperialism Is A Paper Tiger", July 14, 1956 https://www.marxists.org.

[238] Sun-Ki Chai, "An Organizational Economics Theory of Antigovernment Violence", *Comparative Politics* 26(1) (1993): 99-110; Bonnie Cordes et al., "Trends in International Terrorism, 1982 and 1983", DTIC Document, 1984, https://apps.dtic.mil;Martha Crenshaw, "Theories of Terrorism: Instrumental and Organizational Approaches", *Journal of Strategic Studies* 10, 4 (1987): 13–31; Thomas Schelling, "What Purposes Can International Terrorism Serve?", in: Gillespie Frey and Christopher Morris (ed.) *Violence, Terrorism, and Justice*, New York: Cambridge University Press, 1991, pp. 18-32.

[239] David A. Lake, "Rational Extremism: Understanding Terrorism in the Twenty-First Century", Dialogue *IO* 1(1) (2002): 15-29; Harvey E. Lapan and Todd Sandler, "Terrorism and Signaling", *European Journal of Political Economy* 9(3) (1993): 383-397; Ethan Bueno de Mesquita, "The Terrorist Endgame A Model with Moral Hazard and Learning", *Journal of Conflict Resolution* 49(2) (2005): 237-258; Per Baltzer Overgaard, "The Scale of Terrorist Attacks as a Signal of Resources",

Journal of Conflict Resolution 38(3) (1994): 452-478.

[240] Yagil Henkin, "How to Win Small Wars", Azur, Summer, 24, 2006.

http://tchelet.org.il Bruce Hoffman, "The Rationality of Terrorism and Other Forms of Political Violence: Lessons from the Jewish Campaign in Palestine, 1939- 1947", *Small Wars and Insurgencies* 22(2) (2011): 258-272; Wilkinson, Terrorism versus Democracy.

[241] Aaron Edwards, "Abandoning Armed Resistance? The Ulster Volunteer Force as a Case Study of Strategic Terrorism in Northern Ireland", *Studies in Conflict and Terrorism* 32(2) (2009): 146-166.

242 Dipak K. Gupta, *Understanding Terrorism and Political Violence: The Life Cycle of Birth, Growth, Transformation, and Demise*, London and New-York: Routledge, 2008.

243 Limor Novel, "Is Terrorism Effective? Examining Terrorism Strategy in Achieving Political Goals", Political Sciences Department Bar-Ilan University, 2010.

244 Andrew H. Kydd and Barbara F. Walter, "The Strategies of Terrorism", *International Security* 31(1) (2006): 49-80; Andrew Kydd and Barbara F. Walter, "Sabotaging the Peace: The Politics of Extremist Violence", *International Organization* 56(2) (2002): 263-296.

245 Alan M. Dershowitz, *Why Terrorism Works: Understanding the Threat, Responding to the Challenge*, New Haven and London: Yale University Press, 2002.

246 Goldman, Ogen S. "Between self-interest and international norms: legitimizing the PLO." *Israel Affairs* 19, no. 2 (2013): 364-378.

247 Eric D. Gould and Esteban F. Klor, "Does Terrorism Work?", *The Quarterly Journal of Economics* 125(4) (2010): 1459-1510.

248 Abrahms, "The Political Effectiveness of Terrorism Revisited" 321; Max Abrahms, "Does Terrorism Really Work? Evolution in the Conventional Wisdom since 9/11", *Defense and Peace Economics* 22(6)(2011): 583-594 .

249 Another study which examined violent and non-violent revolts found that in 323 cases between the years 1900-2006, the avoidance of violent revolts was related to the government's compromise with the rebels.

250 Page Fortna, "Do Terrorists Win? Rebels' Use of Terrorism and Civil War Outcomes", Unpublished Manuscript: Department of Political Science, Columbia University, 2011. http://www.princeton.edu.

[251] Two studies found that most terrorist organizations failed to achieve their goals. In one of them only 4 terrorist organizations out of 27 were classified in the category of success. However, at the time of the review some of the organizations were still active and it is impossible to know how the conflict will end. Also, the choice of cases was not sufficiently reasoned. In another study, Max Abrams examined 24 organizations declared terrorist organizations by the United States. Only 3 of them (7%) managed to achieve their goals, even if it was only a partial success. Abram's conclusion was that compared to guerrilla movements, that unlike terrorist organizations aimed their attacks mainly against security forces, they fulfilled fewer of their goals.

Gupta, *Understanding Terrorism and Political Violence*, pp. 189-190. Max Abrahms, "Why Terrorism Does Not Work", *International Security* 31(2) (2006): 42-78.

Audrey Cronin examined 450 terrorist organizations that operated from 1968 to 2006 and found that only 6.4% of them achieved all or most of their goals; A similar percentage has partially achieved its goals. Even when she examined only the organizations, which were declared as terrorist organizations by the United States, she found a similar finding: none of them had achieved their goals in full. It should be noted that Cronin omitted terrorist organizations that operated only once or organizations that did not cause deaths (close to half of the organizations.) So, the rate of successful organizations is much lower because she says (unsurprisingly) none of these organizations have achieved its goals. If Cronin would add these organizations, the rate of successful terrorist organizations was even lower.

Cronin, *How Terrorism Ends*, pp. 208-216.

Seth Jones and Martin Libicki documented 648 terrorist organizations which were active in 1968-2006. They analyzed only organizations that had ceased operations and sifted through organizations that had ceased to function due to a split. The study findings were like those of Cronin's research: only about 10% of the organizations (27) won their struggle.

Jones and Libicki, *How Terrorist Groups End.*

Ariel Merri also found that out of 800 Terrorist organizations, only a few organizations were able to achieve their goals, and they were the organizations that waged anti-colonial wars. His explanation is that in colonial wars the colonial power does not fight for its independence or for its homeland, and therefore the interests of the demanding rebels for independence is stronger than the interests of the powers therefore the probability of achieving political goals is higher.

Ariel Merari, "Terrorism as a Strategy of Insurgency," *Terrorism and Political Violence* 5(4) (1993): 213-251.

[252]Max Abrahms and Karolina Lula, "Why Terrorists Overestimate the Odds of Victory", *Perspectives on Terrorism* 6(4-5) (2012): 46-62.

[253]Sprinzak, "Rational Fanatics," p. 66.

[254] Robert A. Pape, "The Strategic Logic of Suicide Terrorism," *American Political Science Review* 97(3) (2003): 343-361; Pape, Dying to Win; Sprinzak, "Rational Fanatics".

[255] For the opposite view, which negates the effectiveness of suicide terrorism see: Max Abrahms, "Dying for Nothing? The Political Ineffectiveness of Suicide Terrorism", in: Stuart Gottlieb (ed.), *Debating Terrorism Counterterrorism*, Washington D.C: Congressional Quarterly, 2010, pp.147-167.

[256] Pape, "The Strategic Logic of Suicide Terrorism," pp. 9-10, 329.

[257] Pape, p. 14.

[258] Assaf Moghadam also mentioned several criticisms about Pipe's analysis. For example, Pipe removed from the list of suicide

bombings 5 cases that have not yet ended while conducting the study. Precisely these five cases were about three times longer than the other suicide terrorism campaigns. Pipe also claimed that Hamas' suicide attacks in 1994 spurred Israel to hand over territory to the Palestinians. This claim does not stand the test of reality, as Hamas in fact opposed the Oslo Accords and carried out its attacks to stop the political process not to accelerate it and cause Israel to withdraw from territories.

Assaf Moghadam, "Suicide Terrorism, Occupation, and the Globalization of Martyrdom: A Critique of Dying to Win", *Studies in Conflict and Terrorism* 29(8) (2006): 707-729.

[259] Abrahms, "The Political Effectiveness of Terrorism Revisited".

[260] It is advisable to qualify this conclusion, since in the studies mentioned here the analysis used data only until the year 2003 and since then has passed more than a decade, in which many other cases of suicide terrorism have occurred.

[261]This subsection does not examine the effectiveness of counter-terrorism measures, for example:

Audrey Cronin and Kurt Ludes, eds., "Introduction: Meeting and Managing the Threat," in: *Attacking Terrorism: Elements of a Grand Strategy*, 2004, pp. 1–2; Cynthia Lum, Leslie W. Kennedy, and Alison Sherley, "Are Counter-Terrorism Strategies Effective? The Results of the Campbell Systematic Review on Counter-Terrorism Evaluation Research", *Journal of Experimental Criminology* 2(4) (2006): 489-516; Edward H. Kaplan et al., "What Happened to Suicide Bombings in Israel? Insights from a Terror Stock Model", *Studies in Conflict and Terrorism* 28(3) (2005): 225-235.

[262] Idan Dorner, "After A Quarter of Century The Tamil Tigers Surrendered", Walla News 17 May 2009, https://news.walla.co.il

[263] Dorner.

264 This short review on the Liberation Tigers of Tamil Eelam is based on: Shlomi Yas "Sri-Lanka and The Tamil Tigers: Conflict and Legitimation", *Military and Strategy* 2(6) (2014): 65-82; Christine Fair, "Diaspora Involvement in Insurgencies: Insights from the Khalistan and Tamil Eelam Movements", *Nationalism and Ethnic Politics* 11 (2005): 125-156; South Asia Terrorism Portal, "Liberation Tigers of Tamil Eelam (LTTE)", November 1, 2015, http://www.satp.org.

265 For example: Crenshaw, "Theories of Terrorism"; Todd Sandler and Kevin Siqueira, "Global Terrorism: Deterrence versus Pre-Emption", *Canadian Journal of Economics/Revue Canadienne d'économique* 39(4) (2006): 1370-1387; Goldman, Ogen. "The importance of voluntary associations for guerrilla movements." *Studies in Conflict & Terrorism* 36, no. 10 (2013): 789-818.

266 Paul K. Davis and Brian Michael Jenkins, *Deterrence and Influence in Counterterrorism: A Component in the War on Al Qaeda*, Santa Monica: RAND Corporation, 2002; Laura Dugan and Erica Chenoweth, "Moving Beyond Deterrence the Effectiveness of Raising the Expected Utility

of Abstaining from Terrorism in Israel", *American Sociological Review* 77(4) (2012): 597-624; Jan Henryk Pierskalla, "Protest, Deterrence, and Escalation: The Strategic Calculus of Government Repression", *Journal of Conflict Resolution* 54(1) (2010): 117-145; Thomas Rid, "Deterrence beyond the State: The Israeli Experience*", Contemporary Security Policy* 33(1) (2012): 124-147; Robert Trager and Dessislava P. Zagorcheva, "Deterring Terrorism: It Can Be Done," *International Security* 30(3) (2005): 87-123.

267Cronin, "Behind the Curve", p. 55; Cronin and Ludes, "Attacking Terrorism"; Barry R. Posen, "The Struggle against Terrorism: Grand Strategy, Strategy, and Tactics", *International Security* 26(3) (2002): p. 47; Jeffrey Ian Ross and Ted Robert Gurr,

"Why Terrorism Subsides: A Comparative Study of Canada and the United States", *Comparative Politics* 21(4) (1989): 405-426; Trager and Zagorcheva, "Deterring Terrorism"; Wilkinson, Terrorism versus Democracy, pp. 77-79.

268 Nadav Morag, "Measuring Success in Coping with Terrorism: The Israeli Case", *Studies in Conflict and Terrorism* 28(4) (2005): 307-320; Shalom and Hendel, *Let the IDF Win*.

269 Laura Dugan and Erica Chenoweth, "Moving Beyond Deterrence the Effectiveness of Raising the Expected Utility of Abstaining from Terrorism in Israel", *American Sociological Review* 77(4) (2012): 597; Mete Feridun and Muhammad Shahbaz, "Fighting": **624**

More examples: Terrorism: Are Military Measures Effective? Empirical Evidence from Turkey", *Defense and Peace Economics* 21(2) (2010): 193-205.

270 Jones and Libicki, *How Terrorist Groups End*.

271 Gompert et al., War by Other Means – Building Complete and Balanced Capabilities for Counterinsurgency.

272 Fortna, "Do Terrorists Win?".

273 David Mason, Joseph P. Weingarten, and Patrick J. Fett, "Win, Lose, or Draw: Predicting the Outcome of Civil Wars", *Political Research Quarterly* 52(2) (1999): 239-268.

274 Research about rebellions which took place between the years 1946-2008 found that 64% of the rebellions in which unconventional warfare was used ended in the victory of the government, but only 20% ended in victory for the rebels.

Laia Balcells and Stathis N. Kalyvas, "Does Warfare Matter? Severity, Duration, and Outcomes of Civil Wars", *SSRN Scholarly Paper Rochester*, New-York: Social Science Research Network, November 1, http://papers.ssrn.com 2012.

Another study examined 286 uprisings using guerrilla tactics in the years 1800-2005. In this study it was found that in 81% of the cases that occurred before the First World War (1914) the powers defeated the insurgents, and after the war the victory rate was 40%. After World War II the rate of cases won by the government stood at 25%-40%.

Jason Lyall and Isaiah Wilson, "Rage against the Machines: Explaining Outcomes in Counterinsurgency Wars" *International Organization* 63(1) (2009): 67-106.

It should be noted that even in the last decade it seems that governments are succeeding in defeating rebel organizations. The low victory rate does not indicate an increase in victory for the rebels but on an increase in the rate of cases that ended in a draw or in negotiations.

Kalyvas and Balcells, "Does Warfare Matter? Severity, Duration, and Outcomes of Civil Wars".

These findings are reinforced by a study that examined 89 uprisings (about 16 of which were not yet completed at the time of the study), and of the 73 uprisings that remained, the government won about 38% and in about 26% of the uprisings none of the parties achieved their goals in full.

Ben Connable and Martin C. Libicki, *How Insurgencies End*, RAND Corporation, CA: Santa Monica, 2010.

Another study examined 200 asymmetrical wars in the years 1800-2003 and found that after World War II, in 71% of the wars the powerful actor (the state) won. Secondly, to the end of the 20th century the states won about 49% of the asymmetrical wars.

Ivan Arreguín-Toft, *How the Weak Win Wars: A Theory of Asymmetric Conflict*, Cambridge: Cambridge University Press, 2005, pp. 3-4.